FORGING HISTORY

FORGING HISTORY

◆

THE DETECTION OF FAKE
LETTERS & DOCUMENTS

◆

KENNETH W. RENDELL

University of Oklahoma Press ◆ Norman and London

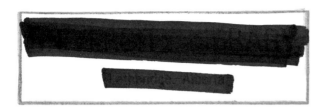

Library of Congress Cataloging-in-Publication Data

Rendell, Kenneth W.
    Forging history : the detection of fake letters & documents /
Kenneth W. Rendell
        p.   cm.
    Includes bibliographical references and index
    ISBN 0-8061-2636-1
    1. History—Errors, inventions, etc. 2. Forgery of manuscripts.
3. Impostors and imposture. I. Title.
D10.R45   1994
909—dc20   94-2098
                                                            CIP

The paper in the book meets the guidelines for permanence and durability
of the Committee on Production Guidelines for Book Longevity
of the Council on Library Resources, Inc.

1 2 3 4 5 6 7 8 9 10

Contents

Acknowledgments

The subject of forgeries has, of necessity, fascinated me for the more than three decades that I have been a dealer in historical letters and documents. Mary Benjamin, the first dealer from whom I bought material, set a high standard in authenticating material, and her expertise gave me, a new collector, great confidence. During the past thirty years, my friend, Charles Hamilton, has frequently entertained me with stories of his personal encounters with forgers. Many of them are recounted in his excellent book, *Famous Forgers*.

The original draft of the present book was reviewed by six friends and colleagues, each with a somewhat different perspective. I am very grateful for their comments and help: Terry Belanger, Roy Davids, Rosalie Fawcett, Charles Hamilton, Shirley McNerney, and Marvin Sadik.

The forgeries illustrated are from my personal collection of forgeries, unless otherwise noted; the photographs showing enlargements of letters and other writing characteristics were taken by Rosalie Fawcett using the microscope camera illustrated in the chapter on equipment.

Introduction

Virtually since the beginning of writing, people have been trying to affect our knowledge of current events, our history, and our literature by forging the principal means by which such information is conveyed to us — letters, manuscripts, documents, and diaries. The written word, even in this modern era of video, telephone and satellite communication, is the basis of much of today's news, and hence tomorrow's history. The forging of manuscript material has most commonly been done to change history rather than for financial gain.

The most famous modern forgery cases, most notably the Hitler diaries, have contained elements of both: efforts to change history and swindle money. This book will discuss many of the forgeries created primarily for the purpose of changing history, but it is principally about the forging of documents for financial gain. The latter have generally been the far more sophisticated forgeries, in which the forger has combined research of the texts of the manuscripts with the use of scientific knowledge and extraordinary skill in their physical creation. The former have been the more sophisticated hoaxes involving elaborate provenance and situations wherein the victims of the forgeries end up playing an important role as the proponents of the forgeries and frauds.

Time magazine, in the most authoritative and in-depth article written on the subject by a national publication, commented, "If it were only sexier, it might have rated recognition as the world's oldest profession. Ever since human kind became literate, civilization has been bedeviled by the forger's determination to deceive by mimicking the writing of others" (May 16, 1983).

The histories of the ancient and medieval worlds are complicated by both literary and historical forgeries. The zeal of the Ptolemies in building their libraries created a tremendous demand for the manuscripts of ancient writers, and the forgers of the day were happy to provide them. Numerous literary forgeries were created in the ancient world including letters of Euripides, of Themistocles, and of Socrates; many of these were not uncovered until centuries later. Perhaps the earliest forgery that had a major effect on history was the Donation of Constantine. This document was supposedly in the hand of the Roman emperor Constantine I, who converted to Christianity in A.D. 312. According to this document, the emperor gave the pope dominion over Rome and "all provinces, localities and towns in Italy and the western hemisphere." Constantinople's threat to reduce the importance of Rome and the papacy in the eighth century was abruptly halted with the discovery of this document. When Pope Stephen II produced the document in A.D. 754, he was put in the position of dominating Constantinople, rather than the other way around. Not until the fifteenth century was this document, which had given great authority to the papacy for seven hundred years, shown to be a forgery, done most likely by someone in the papal chancery during the reign of Pope Stephen.

In the late eighteenth century William Henry Ireland forged manuscripts of Shakespeare. Emboldened by the acceptance of his forgeries, he created a new "Shakespeare" play, *Vortigern and Rowena*. This proved to be his undoing. It was one thing to copy the texts of *Hamlet* and *King Lear* on vellum (itself a giveaway, since Shakespeare himself would not have used a material that was almost exclusively reserved for legal documents); it was another to attempt to continue Shakespeare's literary legacy. Like later attempts of forgery for historical or literary purposes, the physical skills in creating these forgeries were rudimentary.

The Franco-Prussian War of 1870 was started when Bismarck altered the report of a meeting between the Prussian king and the French ambassador. Bismarck, wanting to precipitate a war with France, forged the report to make it appear that the Prussian king was insulting the French. When this report was released to the newspapers the enraged French nation accommodated Bismarck by declaring war.

The most notable international case of anti-Semitism, the framing of the French captain, Alfred Dreyfus, was based on forged evidence that he had given away confidential information. Only a few years later the *Protocols of the Elders of Zion* appeared. This purported to be the text of a report of secret meetings of the Elders of Zion in Basel, Switzerland, in which they planned to conquer the world. In reality, the *Protocols* were fabricated by agents of the czar in France and first published in Russia at the end of the nineteenth century. Although an amateurish forgery, it was accepted as true by Wilhelm II and Nicholas II, and a long article in the London *Times* asserted that it appeared genuine and should be taken seriously. Hitler made great use of the *Protocols* in his anti-Semitic attacks.

Thus far in the twentieth century, four major journalistic hoaxes have been based on forged manuscripts or letters. Three of the four were poorly created forgeries.

In 1928, the *Atlantic Monthly* published a series of articles based on forged love letters of Abraham Lincoln to Ann Rutledge. Like the Hitler diaries more than half a century later, several prominent scholars immediately authenticated the letters, among them Carl Sandburg, Lincoln's most famous biographer, and Ida Tarbell, another Lincoln biographer. The letters were absurd forgeries, full of anachronisms; moreover, they were signed with the name Lincoln abhorred— Abe. One of the early supporters of the letters realized that he had been duped by the charms of the woman offering them for publication and withdrew his support as numerous scholars pointed out all of the textual indications of forgery. A forensic examination was apparently never considered before publication.

The diaries of Benito Mussolini, forged in 1957, were contrived with much greater skill: they were authenticated by the dictator's son, Vittorio, and a Swiss expert from Lausanne University. Relying upon logic that only a person who is not a forgery expert would use, a logic later echoed by similar "experts" who examined the Hitler diaries, the man from Lausanne wrote, "Thirty volumes of manuscripts cannot be the work of a forger, but a genius. . . . You can falsify a few lines or even pages, but not a series of diaries." After competent experts examined them and declared them fraudulent, the Italian police seized all but four volumes and charged two women with forgery. They pleaded guilty and were given suspended sentences.

Eleven years later the four remaining Mussolini diaries that the police had not found were sold to the London *Sunday Times* for a substantial sum. Unaware of the history of the diaries, their editors consulted experts who immediately found substantial proof of forgery, and they were never published.

The forging of Howard Hughes's autobiography, unlike previous journalistic hoaxes, was physically very well done. This hoax relied upon Hughes's mania for secrecy and was based on the presumption that the man who had forfeited hundreds of millions of dollars rather than appear in court and testify about his management of TWA would certainly not make a verifiable statement concerning his alleged collaboration with Clifford Irving on his autobiography. Irving and his wife forged a contract with Hughes, correspondence from him discussing the writing of the book, and Hughes's name on checks. This handwriting had been examined by a leading questioned document expert and declared to be genuine. Irving had gained access to a manuscript which contained much inside information about Hughes, information which could have come from only one source, and this was the crack in the well-planned hoax that Irving and his wife had created.

In a completely unanticipated change of attitude Hughes himself also condemned the authenticity of the manuscript, agreeing to be interviewed in a telephone conference by reporters who could verify the speaker's identity. Other questioned document experts declared the writing to be forged, and Swiss authorities were able to identify Irving's wife as the "H.R. Hughes" who had deposited the publisher's checks. Hughes was to be posthumously involved in several more forgery cases, the many forgeries of his will.

The century's most highly publicized forgeries were the Hitler diaries. How these poorly executed forgeries could fool three questioned document experts, how scholars could attest to their historical authenticity, and how journalists could not find the glaring flaws in their provenance is an incredible and fascinating saga.

Perhaps more questions will remain after reading the story of the Mormon forger, con man and bomber, Mark Hofmann. His forgeries, created with great skill and scientific knowledge after months of research into the context of each piece, were intended to rewrite Mormon theology. Yet they were very quickly unmasked. The story of this disillusioned Mormon who wanted to rewrite Mormon history according to what he believed actually did happen is told in chapter 7.

These are the famous cases that have resulted in great media attention; they are not, however, with the exception of the Mormon forger, Mark Hofmann, the cases that have been the most difficult for the expert in historical documents. These famous cases have been better hoaxes than skilled forgeries.

This book is concerned with the forgeries that have been created with the greatest technical skill and textual accuracy, forgeries that have been created to dupe handwriting experts, not journalists, and created to defraud dealers, collectors and curators out of money. They were not usually created by persons who wanted to change history or literature. The expert who is prepared to deal with this type of forger has had, as the previously discussed cases illustrate, little difficulty in unmasking the creator of journalistic hoaxes.

The authentication of autograph material is a painstaking and meticulous procedure for the expert, requiring a thorough knowledge of the characteristics of forged and genuine writing; technical data concerning paper, ink, and writing instruments; the effective methods of comparing handwritings; common habits of forgers; and the necessary equipment for reaching a definitive conclusion. Many of the factors considered in examining handwriting are not conclusive proof of authenticity by themselves and must be evaluated in relation to other evidence. Obvious points, such as paper manufactured after the purported date of the document, instantly indicate a forgery. However, it can be an error to conclude from an examination of only a few factors that the writing is genuine or forged.

Various factors other than forgery can cause a change in a person's handwriting. The two principal ones are age and illness. Handwriting from different periods of a person's life may differ markedly. Unusual circumstances in the way in which a letter or document was written or signed may also give the appearance of forgery. Most people, for example, write a much clearer signature when affixing it to an important legal document than to a routine check; it is an important event, and the signature is usually written with more care. People *sign* their names, in most cases, quite differently from the way in which they would *write* their names (for example, in the text of a letter). This difference becomes a factor if for some reason a person must alter his signature to fit the space available. The resulting signature is frequently written with characters quite different from those used in the person's normal signature, letter formations more characteristic of his writing in the body of a letter.

The illustrations in this book are generally intended to clarify only the point under discussion indicating forgery, although many other points will be evident, particularly as the reader progresses and gains a knowledge of the factors indicating forgery.

It is important to understand the difference between the approach and scope of the "questioned document expert" and that of the expert in historical documents and letters. This distinction became most apparent in the Hitler diaries case, when three leading questioned document experts authenticated pages from the questioned diaries which were, in fact, poor forgeries.

Those who represent themselves by the term "questioned document examiner" are generally concerned with modern contemporary forgeries, usually of persons whose habits and handwriting are barely known to them. Most of their work is involved in testifying in court as to whether or not a check, contract, kidnap note, and so on, was likely to have been written by the person being charged with a crime. Other work involves business disputes over whether contracts have been altered or forged or dating documents created within the past several decades.

The knowledge they have is highly specialized and is mainly related to recent materials. They are rarely asked to work on anything more than a few years old. Their knowledge of ballpoint pens, modern inks and papers, typewriter faces, and other modern materials is far more extensive than that of experts in historical documents and letters.

From my own experiences with such experts, I have been struck by the willingness of some to make a case for either side in a questioned document dispute. There was no shortage of experts to testify on both sides in the several Howard Hughes will cases, and too many seem to have the attitude of being a "hired gun" to advocate a point of view rather than presenting an unbiased scientific analysis.

Experts in authenticating historical letters and documents are mostly dealers in these artifacts. For them a piece is either genuine or not, and if there is any question of its authenticity it cannot be sold. Dealers who act ethically in historical documents and letters put their reputations and their money behind each piece that they buy and sell. Conclusions are not based upon a probability of genuineness; it is not sufficient for most of this evidence to point to the piece being authentic. The evidence must be conclusive or the ethical dealer will not offer it for sale. The dealer in historical letters and documents has a great advantage over his colleagues in the questioned document field — the dealer does not have to reach a conclusion. Unlike the expert hired to reach a conclusion one way or the other, the dealer can simply decline to handle a piece he is not absolutely certain of.

In the case of the Hitler diaries, no competent dealer in historical documents would have accepted examples for comparison from the person who brought them the questioned writing itself. Yet that is exactly what highly regarded questioned document experts did in this case. Dealers are always on the alert for someone trying to defraud them with forgeries. Some questioned document examiners and other professional expert witnesses seem to be too distant from the reality of the impact of their opinions; their attitude is a very impersonal one. It is not impersonal when you have to put your name and money behind every item you sell.

Another major difference between the two groups is the knowledge of the habits and handwriting of individuals who are frequently forged. This knowledge is acquired over many years of buying and selling letters and documents. Any dealer who has bought and sold Adolf Hitler material would know that the dictator (whose military appointments and awards were elaborately and ornately presented) would never have had his own diaries bound in cheap imitation leather. This intimate knowledge of a person's writing, personal habits, and differences in handwriting during different periods of time is of obvious and great importance in detecting historical forgeries.

Collectors are frequently advised to buy only from "reliable and reputable" dealers, but how is a new collector to make such a determination? Most dealers give an unconditional guarantee of authenticity. This guarantee should be unlimited in time — a lifetime guarantee, not a limited one. The piece may be in your collection for years and not subject to any other expert examination until you wish to sell it. Why would any expert confident of his authentication put a time limit on his authentication? It cannot simply change from genuine to forged after a number of years have elapsed.

Ask dealers about their experience — not just in terms of years but also how much similar material they have handled. Ask about articles in scholarly journals, papers delivered before archival and library groups, recognition by their peers of their being experts. But, most important, ask dealers how they authenticated pieces in question.

This book will show you that authentication of historical letters and documents is based neither on "intuition" nor on "gut feelings." Authentication of historical letters and documents uses an analytic approach that can be illustrated and proven. Dealers who cannot explain their methods of authentication to your satisfaction are ones you should avoid.

It is true that an initial element that many call "intuition" does play an important part in any examination of questioned documents; but what is frequently called intuition is a simultaneous observation of combinations of facts reflected against the mental images stored during decades of experience, giving an initial indication of whether the document in question meets the general criteria of genuine documents of the period and circumstances.

When I was shown the twenty-five or so pieces that the Mormon forger was subsequently charged with creating, I was told that only a few were being questioned. In less than half an hour I had concluded that most likely all were forgeries. That could have been described as intuition, but that "intuition" was based on the instinctive observation that the paper "felt" a little different from how it should, the pen lines were a little shaky, ink colors were a little off, styles of handwriting just did not fit with thousands of letters I had seen from the same period and geographical area over the past thirty years. In only another ten minutes, however, I had found one scientific error that the Mormon forger had made — a common denominator that could be demonstrated in court, not a subjective opinion but a factor that would graphically and conclusively demonstrate to a jury that these were forgeries.

That is what this book is all about — how an expert can conclusively prove, and demonstrate, that a historical document is genuine or a forgery.

1

General Characteristics of Forged Writing

The most immediately apparent characteristics of forged writing are its drawn or labored appearance and slow hesitating strokes intermingled with shaky strokes, frequently exhibiting far too much attention to detail and too much care in the formation of individual letters. The forgery of Calvin Coolidge [1] shows many changes in writing the two capital *C*'s as well as a drawn appearance. These characteristics are all a result of attempting to imitate someone else's writing patterns rather than instinctively following one's own. Normal writing is written with speed, flow and smoothness, without interruption and with a lack of attention to detail and individual letter formations. (There are, of course, exceptions, particularly in the case of illness or advanced age.)

The forged George Washington letter [2] is reasonably well done, but when compared with a genuine Washington autograph letter [3], the shaky strokes and excessive care taken in the writing become immediately apparent. The forged letter of Grover Cleveland [5] and the musical manuscript of Richard Wagner [7] as well as the signature of Calvin Coolidge [1] demonstrate this tendency.

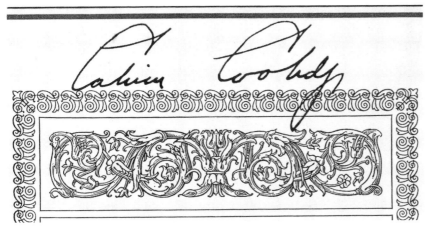

1 A forged signature of Calvin Coolidge
   written with meticulous care, resulting
   in shaky strokes

G Washington [signature]

Mount Vernon May 16th 1785:

Dear Sir,

In for a penny, in for a pound is an old adage.—I am so hackneyed to the touches of the Painters pencil, that I am now altogether at their beck, and sit like patience on a Monument whilst they are delineating the lines of my face.—

It is a proof among many others, of what habit & custom can effect.—at first I was as impatient at the request, and as restive under the operation, as a Colt is of the Saddle—The next time, I submitted very reluctantly, but with less flouncing.—Now, no dray moves more readily to the Thill, than I do to the Painters Chair.—It may easily be conceived therefore that I yielded a ready obedience to your request, and to the views of Mr. Pine.

Letters from England, recommendatory of this Gentleman, came to my hand previous to his arrival in America—not only as an Artist of acknowledged eminence, but as one who had discovered a friendly disposition towards this Country for which, it seems, he had been marked.

It gave me pleasure to hear from you—I shall always feel an interest in your happiness—and with Mrs. Washingtons compliments & best wishes joined to my own, for Mrs. Hopkinson & yourself.

I am—Dr. Sir,
Yr. most Obedt. & affectd.
Hble Servant
G Washington

Frans. Hopkinson Esqr.

2 A forged letter of George Washington written with characteristic shaky and drawn strokes

Mount Vernon Aug. 18th 1788.

Sir;

      Your congratulatory letter, on the adoption of the Constitution by the Convention of New York, has been placed in my hands: and I have in return, to request that you will be assured it would be incompatible with the feelings of the good Citizens of America to be insensible to the friendly sentiments, expressed by patriotic foreigners for their public felicity. — For myself, it might be superfluous to add more than that I remain with due impressions for your partiality in my favour,

      Sir, Yr. most obedient &
      most Hble Servant

      G. Washington

The Marquis
      de Lotbinière

3 A genuine autograph letter of George Washington
dated August 18, 1788

EXECUTIVE MANSION,
WASHINGTON.

[handwritten letter]

4 A genuine letter of Grover Cleveland
dated March 23, 1896

well
expressed or in the least lose
their potency and influence.
Surely if English
speech supplies the token of
united effort for the good
of mankind and the impulse
of an exalted international
mission we do well to
fittingly honor the name and
memory of William Shakespeare.
Yours very truly
Grover Cleveland

Hon George F. Parker
President &c

5 A forged letter of Grover Cleveland
with a very drawn appearance

6 A genuine letter of Richard Wagner
dated March 19, 1876

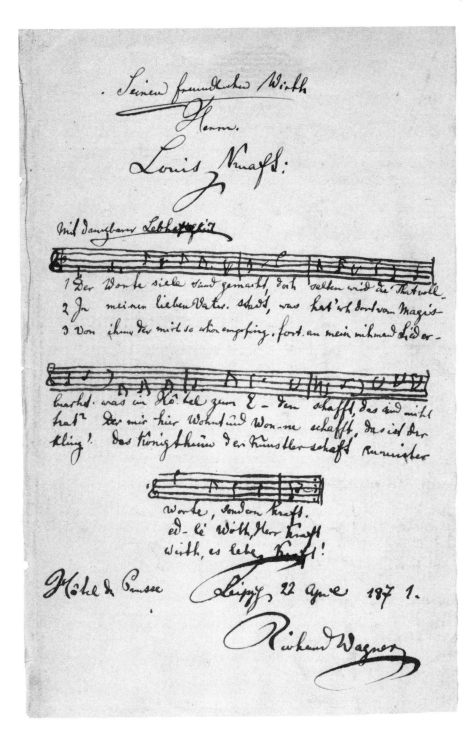

7 A forged letter of Richard Wagner
written with very shaky strokes

Forged Civil War signatures
and a forged signature of
George Bernard Shaw

The group of Civil War signatures and the signature of George Bernard Shaw below also show the shaky lines and telltale drawn appearance of forgeries. Additionally, they illustrate the fact that not all forgeries are created for financial or literary reasons. These examples, of relatively little value, were probably forged while the purported authors were living and collectors competed with each other to obtain their autographs [8].

The care taken in executing forgeries will often produce signatures that are much more legible than genuine examples. This characterististic is demonstrated in the following illustrations.

9a Genuine signatures

9b Forged signatures

George Washington

Benjamin Franklin

Charles Dickens

Richard Wagner

10a-c
Forged writing showing that the forgers have not moved their pens rapidly onto and off of the surface of the paper, thereby leaving heavier concentrations of ink at the beginnings and ends of strokes

11a-c
Genuine writing showing the effect of flying starts and endings

Normal genuine writing begins and ends with what can be called flying starts and endings; the initial stroke commences as a very fine line, broadening as it approaches the initial formation of the character. The writer terminates the writing by rapidly removing the pen from the surface of the paper, resulting in a final stroke that decreases in width until it disappears [11a-c]. While this is not necessarily true of all writers, few people begin writing by boldly putting the pen onto the paper directly and then beginning the stroke. Nor do they hesitate after finishing the final stroke and then lift the pen directly off the paper [10a-c]. This method of writing is, however, very common among forgers, who, of course, are not writing in a normal manner. The effect of placing the pen directly onto the paper and lifting it directly off is shown in the following illustrations.

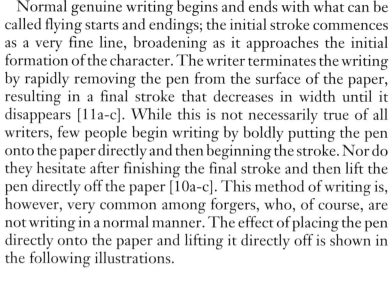

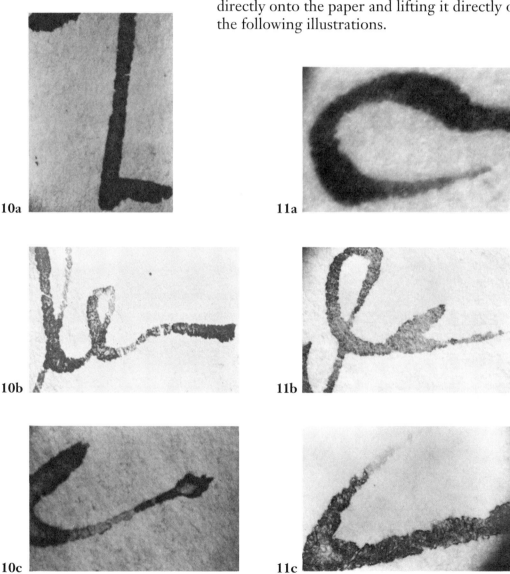

10a

11a

10b

11b

10c

11c

No knowledge of how Greta Garbo, Clark Gable, or Vivien Leigh actually signed their names is necessary to identify the consistent blunt endings and frequent blunt starts that alerted experts to the probability of forgery in these and other examples [12-15]. The California forger who created them was briefly successful in selling to movie memorabilia collectors, but his fraud was short-lived. The photographs were originals, easily obtainable from various dealers who offer original movie stills for sale.

12 A movie still of Greta Garbo with a forged inscription and signature

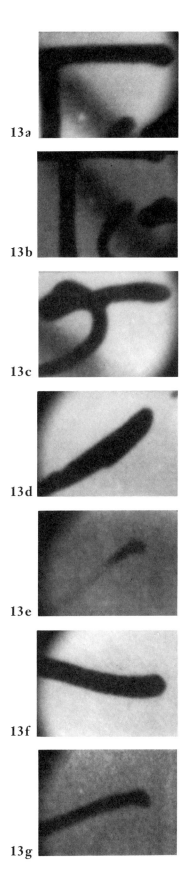

13a

13b

13c

13d

13e

13f

13g

13a-g
Enlargements of letters from the Garbo photo showing blunt starts and endings

14 A movie still from *Gone with the Wind* with forged inscriptions of Clark Gable and Vivien Leigh

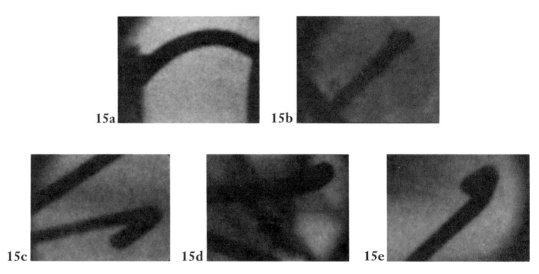

15a-e Enlargements of letters from the still showing blunt starts and endings

Lifting the pen when writing individual letters has been the habit of some less accomplished forgers, and unless it is known that the author of the writing in question had this habit, such pen lifts can instantly unmask forgeries. The more skillful forger can align the continuing stroke after a pen lift, but in many cases the ink from the continuing stroke will flow back onto the first stroke, creating a double thickness of ink. (Ballpoint pens, particularly the early models, and pencils create writing in which pen lifts are virtually impossible to detect.)

Rewriting or retouching is unusual in genuine writing and is done only to make it more legible. Great care is not normally taken by the writer. If a pen runs out of ink, or otherwise fails, a writer will begin again where the quality of the writing was affected. Rewriting or retouching which shows an intention of continuing a smooth form, in the absence of ink depletion, should always be a signal of a possible forgery. The *h* in George Washington's signature has clearly been retouched after the pen was lifted off the writing surface [16, 17].

A significant number of writers do not use the same form of capital letters in their writing as they do in their signatures. Their signatures have more stylized, more individual capitals, and many forgers have used the signature form of a capital in the body of the text. This was one of the glaring errors of Konrad Kujau, the forger of the Hitler diaries. With little of Hitler's genuine handwriting to study, Kujau wrote all of the capital *H*'s in the text with the highly stylized *H* from Hitler's signature, when in fact Hitler always employed a very plain *H* in the body of his writing [18].

Tracings are infrequently encountered in the field of historical documents, but they do occur. Those made by placing paper over a genuine signature and using transmitted light to project the image are rarely seen, since they require that both the genuine example and the forgery be written on translucent paper, which would be suspect in itself. A more common method is to use a facsimile or photocopy of a genuine signature, placing it over the paper to be forged and with a sharp instrument tracing the genuine facsimile, resulting in an indented line on the blank paper. This indented line is then filled in with ink, but traces of it are nearly impossible to erase and this is a relatively crude method. Equally inept are traced signatures initially done with pencil and then with ink; the pencil markings are later erased. Microscopic examination will show signs of both the indented line and the pencil tracing. The poor line quality of such tracings, however, rarely necessitates such a detailed examination.

16 A forged signature of George Washington revealing evidence of retouching

17 An enlargement of the letter *h* in "Washington" showing the retouching

18 The letter *H* was written in a straight-forward manner by Adolf Hitler (above); the forger has used the stylized form of the letter Hitler used

The most unusual and well executed tracing I have encountered is the signed photograph of Winston Churchill [19]. The ink of the "signature" is bold and heavy, and it is written fairly smoothly. When placed on a light table, with transmitted light from the back, it is immediately apparent that the forger has simply used a heavy ink to write over a printed signature [20].

19
A postcard photograph of Winston Churchill with a printed signature that has been traced over in ink

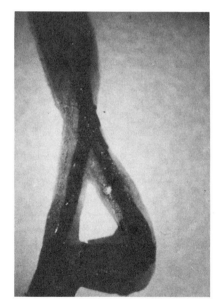

20 An enlargement of Churchill's middle initial *S* showing the tracing

Another characteristic that I have found surprisingly common is the forger's habit of using the same form of writing when forging sections supposedly written by different persons. Dockets and endorsements or other notations that would have been written by the recipient will sometimes contain identical word formations. Some years ago I was offered a document purportedly signed by Thomas Lynch, a signer of the Declaration of Independence whose signature is very rare. The document had an excellent forgery of Lynch's signature, but the owner could not be convinced until I noticed that the document on the verso, supposedly in the hand of the recipient and not by Lynch, was written in the identical and distinctive style of the signer! The forger did not think to adopt a different writing style when acting as the recipient.

A more recent forgery illustrating the same error is the letter purportedly written by Clyde Barrow and signed by him and Bonnie Parker. Having varied the two capital letters, the forger has written "Parker" in Bonnie Parker's signature in the same style as the body of the letter, which was supposedly written by Clyde Barrow [21].

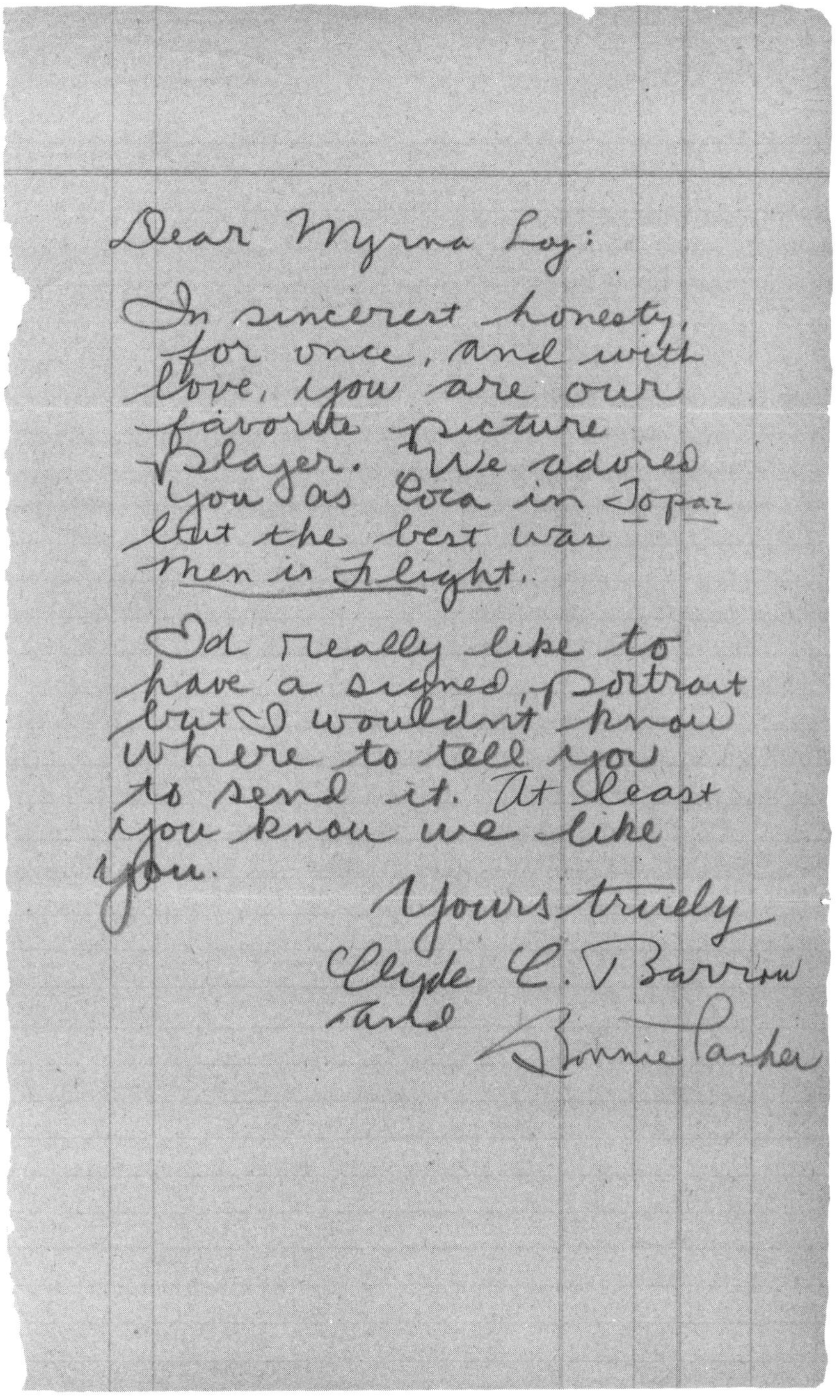

Dear Myrna Loy:

In sincerest honesty,
for once, and with
love, you are our
favorite picture
player. We adored
you as Coca in Topaz
but the best was
Men in Flight..

I'd really like to
have a signed portrait
but I wouldn't know
where to tell you
to send it. At least
you know we like
you.

                Yours truely
            Clyde C. V Barrow
            and
                    Bonnie Parker

21 A forged letter purportedly written by Clyde Barrow and signed
by him and Bonnie Parker. The last name, "Parker," however,
has been written in the same style as that of the text, which is
purported to be in the hand of Clyde Barrow

Sections of forged writing added to genuine documents are usually detected if the forgery was added sometime later, as is usually the case, by the feathering effect of writing on old, porous paper (this is discussed in detail in chapter 2 under the heading "Ink"). Another factor to consider is if the person would have signed such a document [22]. For example, there is no apparent reason for Samuel L. Clemens to have signed the shipping document below. One must also be alert to the possibility that the genuineness of the document does not necessarily authenticate the writing that makes it valuable. The Button Gwinnett signature added to a genuine eighteenth-century account book is forged [23], as is the stylized signature of Frederic Remington and the sketch of a bucking horse added to a page that does bear genuine writing of the American western artist [24, 25].

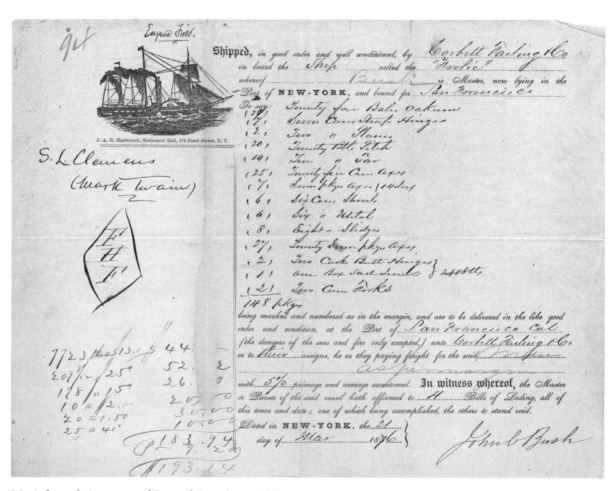

22 A forged signature of Samuel Langhorne Clemens added sometime later to a genuine shipping document dated March 21, 1876

23
A forged signature of Button
Gwinnett added to a genuine
eighteenth-century account book

24 A forged drawing of a bucking horse and signature of Frederic Remington
added to a page bearing genuine writing by the artist

25 On the verso of the Remington forgery is an additional forged drawing and notations.

26
A genuine statement of authenticity by
Eugene Field II, written on the verso of the
Clemens forgery [22]

Some contemporary authentications, such as those by
Eugene Field II, are clear indications of forgery [26]. (The
authentication by Field, dated March 1, 1937, is from the
verso of the Clemens forgery illustrated on page 16.) Other
notes, such as the one added to the group of forged signatures
which includes that of Clemens, were added by the forger for
an authentic look [27], as was the additional endorsement of
Lincoln's law partner, William H. Herndon, on the letter to
Joseph C. Gillespie [28].

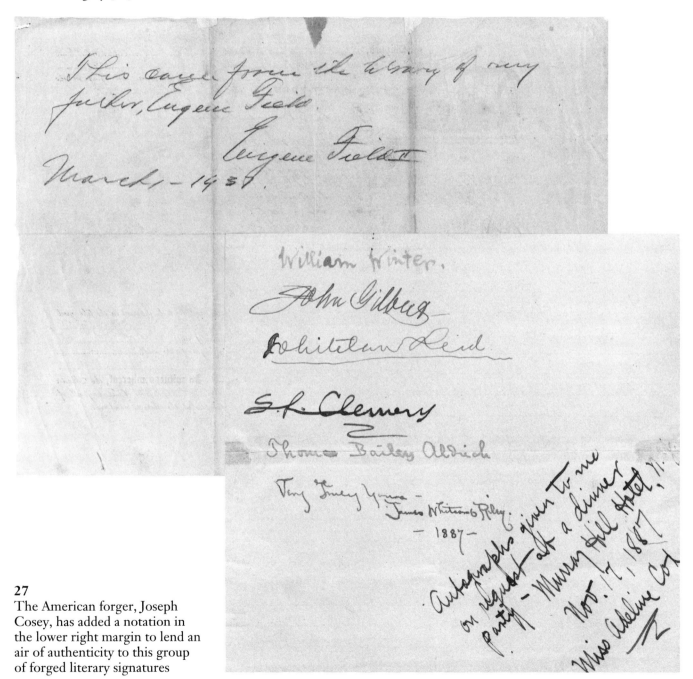

27
The American forger, Joseph
Cosey, has added a notation in
the lower right margin to lend an
air of authenticity to this group
of forged literary signatures

Springfield, June 2nd. 1856

Jos. C. Gillespie, Esq.

My dear Sir,

Here is a copy of an opinion in the Williams case which I sent to the Clerk of Sangamon Court to-day— I do not think that S. T. Logan will agree to his client paying one cent until the court (Davis) decides the issue of the Declaration of March 10th—

I shall welcome your opinion on the matter as you had a similar case last year—

Yours Truly

A. Lincoln

There is a precedent in a similar case in Ohio 14- 372 Wilson vs Ohio R.R. 1847. The Ohio Supreme Court decided in favor of defendants' right to cut and float timber

Wm H. Herndon
June 2 1856

Lincoln's law partner for 19 years

28 A forged endorsement of William H. Herndon, Lincoln's law partner, added to this forged letter of Lincoln, dated June 2, 1856

19

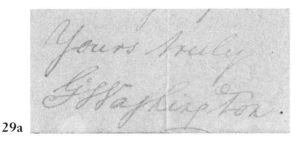

29a

29b

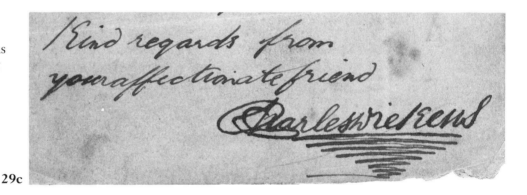

29c

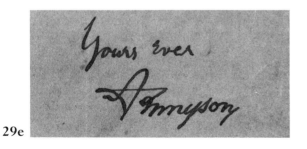

29d

29e

Another consideration in examining the writing alone is consistency of style and form with national characteristics of writing systems of the time. The system of forming letters, linking the characters, and spacing varies widely between countries and periods of time. A system of writing that was common in the United States during the early nineteenth century would be most suspect if it were employed in a letter supposedly written by a native German living in his own country at that time.

Terminology, forms of address, salutations, closings, and the general layout and folding of letters have all changed significantly through the years, and a detailed knowledge of these factors is very important in examining historical documents and letters. The five examples of George Washington, Charles Dickens, and Lord Tennyson all indicate that the forgers had no idea of the genuine terminology of the time [29a-e]. The forger of the Washington letter might as well have written the closing, "Have a Nice Day, George."

Joseph Cosey (1887-ca. 1940s), one of America's most skillful forgers, made his most serious errors in layout. Having developed an ability to imitate Abraham Lincoln's handwriting quite well, Cosey never realized that Lincoln wrote responses and endorsements on the verso of letters to him, rarely on the front, and a note from Lincoln referring the letter to another for action, appearing beneath the text written to him, is very unusual.

The text or content of the letter or document, that is, the facts stated, is of great importance in uncovering forgeries. In many cases it is the content that immediately unmasks them. Forgers have actually dated letters and documents after the death of the supposed author. An important exception to this are presidential documents that were signed in blank and then filled in and dated later. It is therefore possible to have a presidential document dated after the death of the president or after his administration ended. Another exception exists in situations where checks were dated ahead of the day they were written, with the writers of the checks dying before the date of those checks. An example of this occurred when Charles Dickens wrote a check dated June 10, 1870, in payment of his estranged wife's quarterly allowance but died the day before the date of the check, on June 9. Facts, in addition to the date, should be verified — was it likely the writer was in the stated city at that time, are the facts in the text accurate, is it likely the person would have written a letter with this specific content at this time in his life. (George Washington writing in 1797 praising the wisdom of the Louisiana Purchase of 1804 would be a clear sign of forgery!)

The content of the letter or document is not only a major area to examine in terms of forgery, it is also one of the two principal areas of examination to determine if the real person wrote the item in question [the other is handwriting comparison]. There were, for example, many people in Boston at the end of the eighteenth century named Samuel Adams and John Adams, but of the dozens bearing the same name, it is unlikely that they would have written similar letters or signed similar documents as those the patriots did, excluding, of course, routine personal notes. (In these cases, exacting comparisons of handwriting are necessary.)

In the case of the Hitler diaries, the greatest failings were not made by the journalists but by the historians whom they had hired and upon whom they had relied. These historians had access to the content of the diaries long before publication but failed to discover, as other historians later did, that there were no facts in the diaries which were not contained in either a privately printed book by Max Domarus entitled *Hitler: Speeches and Proclamations, 1932-1945* or *Volkischer Beobachter*, the Nazi party's daily newspaper. The diaries even repeated a typographical error, in addition to copying factual errors from the Domarus book.

2

The Materials: Paper, Ink, and Writing Instruments

PAPER

Examination of the paper or parchment can readily unmask many forgeries. A substantial number of forgers have neglected the importance of the paper in dating letters and manuscripts and have used types of paper that were not yet or no longer in use at the time of the purported document. Prior to 1300 parchment or vellum, made from animal skin, was used almost exclusively (papyri and other ancient materials pre-date the scope of the present work). Documents written on paper and dated before the fourteenth century are very unlikely to be genuine — certainly great care would need to be taken in accepting them as authentic. Paper made from linen rags and made on a wire frame (which creates the grid pattern and is given the name "laid" paper) was used concurrently with vellum after 1400, the paper being used almost exclusively for letters and routine matters such as bookkeeping, and the vellum for documents [30]. The use of vellum for important documents continued well into the nineteenth century, and a modern version is still encountered in some unusual cases today. Laid paper has also continued in use until the present time, especially for fine quality writing paper. Wove paper without the grid pattern came into use in America beginning about 1800 and in Europe about 1755 [31]. In 1867, wood pulp paper was commercially introduced; the acidity of this paper varies, but it is generally far less stable than paper made from cloth rags.

An examination of the type of paper used provides a range of possible dates. Some papers are watermarked with a decorative design or the name of the maker and sometimes also with the date of the manufacture of the paper mold on which the paper was made. While it may seem unlikely that a forger would fail to notice a dated watermark, it does happen. A well-written forgery of John F. Kennedy's famous quotation from his inaugural address, "Ask not what your country can do for you, ask what you can do for your country," was written on

30 Laid paper showing a grid pattern of evenly spaced, parallel chain lines

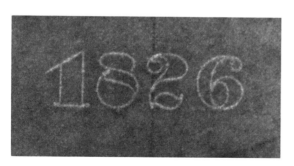

31 Wove paper with the date *1826* for its watermark

genuine White House stationery watermarked 1981, eighteen years after the president's assassination. The skill of the forger did not extend to the common sense of holding the blank piece of White House stationery up to the light.

Undated watermarks can also give evidence of the date of manufacture [32]; to trace them it is necessary to refer to the several standard reference works, notably, *A Catalogue of American Watermarks, 1690-1835* by Thomas L. Gravell and George Miller, *Watermarks in Paper in Holland, England, France, etc., in the XVII and XVIII Centuries* by W. A. Churchill, and the classic work by Charles M. Briquet, *Les Filigranes, Dictionnaire Historique des Marques du Papier des leur Apparition vers 1282 jusque'en 1600.*

The skillful forger, however, can obtain the correct paper of the period without too much difficulty. Contemporary journals and account books with blank pages and the unused leaves of contemporary letters provide the sophisticated forger with his basic materials. The forger of the Mormon documents, Mark Hofmann, for example, obtained the right paper by buying single-page letters with an integral address leaf and separating the letter, leaving a blank page for his forgery. In other cases he removed blank end leaves from contemporary books in libraries, the common resort of nineteenth-century European forgers.

Particular sizes of paper were used during different periods, as were different colors, and size and color can provide the

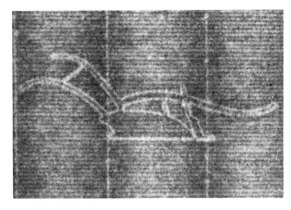

32 Laid paper with a watermark of a plow, the mark of JG & Co/Brandywine, Delaware, made in 1788

33 A forgery of a George Washington receipt inappropriately written on vellum

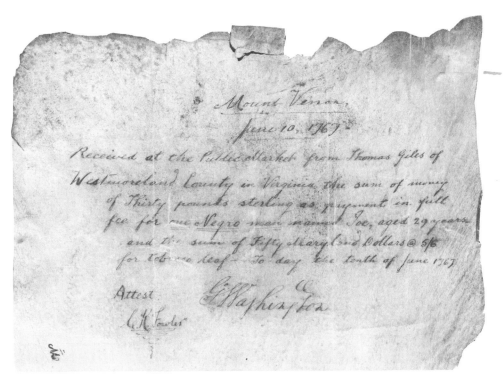

34 A forgery of a letter purportedly by Abraham Lincoln written on imitation vellum

initial clue to a forgery. Oblong folio vellum was the most popular size for documents prior to 1600, as was legal folio paper (about 8-1/2 by 14 inches) for letters. In the late seventeenth century, quarto (approximately 8-1/2 by 11 inches) became the most popular size for letters, with legal documents frequently being written on larger sheets or membranes of vellum. Octavo sizes (about 8 by 6 inches) for letters became common in the early part of the nineteenth century. A glance at the George Washington forgery of a receipt dated June 10, 1767, indicates that the forger was unaware that Washington would not have written a document of this type on vellum, nor would such a small and damaged piece have been used [33]. The Lincoln forgery of the letter dated March 9, 1856, would never have been written on vellum, and this forger has compounded his mistake by using imitation vellum for his forgery [34].

One of the curious aspects of forgery is the false aging of the paper or vellum. While the skillful forger obtains paper contemporary with the period, the amateur attempts to duplicate aged paper by soaking it in tea, burning it, tearing small holes in it, rubbing dirt into the fibers, or by other cosmetic means [35]. When he writes on the paper, the amateur forger invariably avoids the holes and particles of dirt [36]. A slightly less amateurish forger obtains paper that actually is old and follows some of the same "aging" processes

24

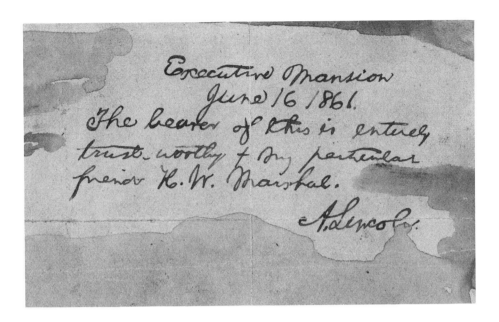

35
A Lincoln forgery written on paper
that has been artificially aged

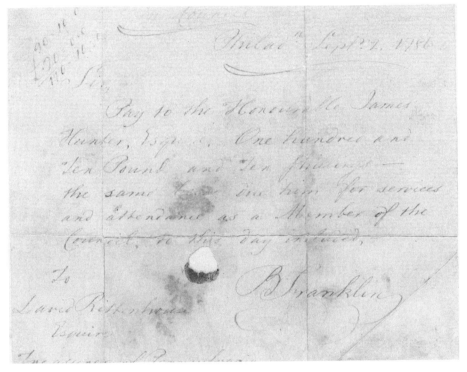

36
A forgery of a Benjamin Franklin
document in which the forger has
written around the hole in the
paper

to avoid having the paper look too new. These forgers are
unaware that most historical letters and documents are in fine
condition (especially when written on laid paper) and that
persons normally wrote letters and documents on paper that
was in excellent condition, without holes or other defects. A
significant exception to this general statement are the holes
that can naturally appear in parchment or vellum documents.
These holes are caused by natural defects in the animal skin
and are not the result of damage or deterioration. Parchment
with these holes already present was used by scribes; they

naturally avoided the holes when writing the text, and legal and business documents are sometimes encountered with these natural characteristics.

Chemical tests of paper are very useful when examining paper made during the past thirty years, a period in which many new chemical combinations have been used in paper-making. Like the chemical analysis of ink, this is a very complex area, and this type of examination of paper is undertaken by specialists in paper analysis. Determining whether paper contains an optical brightener, however, which indicates the paper is post-1950, can be readily done with a good high-intensity ultraviolet light. The optical brightener fluoresces a brilliant white and is unmistakable in showing that the paper was produced after 1950. Many manufacturers have altered watermarks and other patterns so that the year of manufacture can be determined. Some makers of account books, for example, have varied very slightly the width of the columns so that backdated ledgers can be detected.

Anyone examining forgeries of historical documents must be aware of the large numbers of unused genuine printed forms that have been, and are, available to forgers. During the final days of World War II, as allied soldiers raced through Germany, large quantities of unused printed forms and stationery were taken as souvenirs. Unused stationery of Adolf Hitler, embossed in gold with his name and the Nazi eagle, are occasionally sold in the ephemera markets. The genuineness of the paper and printing is, therefore, only one factor in determining authenticity [37].

37
A piece of unused stationery of Adolf Hitler; similar ones have sometimes been filled out by forgers

INK

An examination of the ink is important for determining the earliest date that a letter or document could have been written. As with paper, there are relatively few types of ink to be concerned with until very recent times, when the subject becomes much more complex, and it is necessary to analyze inks chemically to differentiate the many different types of compounds and their dates of use.

The earliest ink was made from finely ground carbon; it was extremely stable and did not attack the vellum or paper. Iron gall ink, the type most often encountered in collecting, was invented in the Middle Ages; it was likely to be acidic in content and to attack the paper. Iron gall also changed color with time, and the reddish tones acquired by many inks of this type are very distinctive and almost impossible to imitate. Equally difficult to imitate is the effect of the high acidity of this type of ink on paper, as is evidenced in the signature on a genuine Robert Morris document written just after the American Revolution. The ink has literally eaten through the paper, leaving only an outline of where some of the writing was [38].

Coloring matter was found in iron gall ink as early as the American Revolution, although this is quite unusual. Colored inks did become increasingly popular, particularly in Europe, after 1835. Indigo, with its characteristic bluish tint, was more commonly added to iron gall ink after 1836 but can be encountered prior to this date. Iron nut gall ink, invented in 1836, differs from other inks, particularly iron gall, in that a considerable part of the coloring matter is held in suspension and as a result penetrates the fibers of the paper rather than drying on the surface.

The year 1856 was significant from the collector's standpoint, since that is when aniline inks were invented. The chief characteristic of this ink is its solubility in water, with the result that the ink will run on contact with water; the primary advantage was that it did not attack the paper as iron gall ink did.

India ink has a uniformity of shading that is comparable to printer's ink, and it is frequently confused with the latter. The sheen of India ink is one means of differentiating between this ink and the dull finish of printer's ink; another is the fact that India ink is waterbased whereas printer's ink is oilbased, a difference that is easy to spot under analysis.

38 Writing from a genuine Robert Morris signature on a document, illustrating the corrosion of paper caused by highly acidic iron gall ink, an effect that is difficult for forgers to duplicate

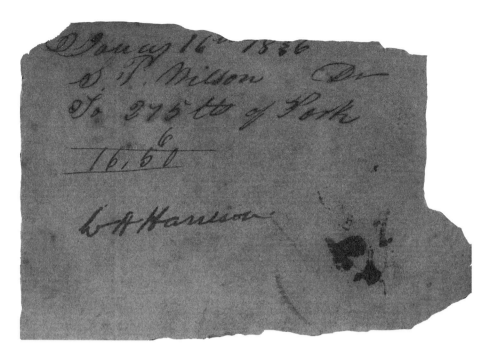

39 A forgery of William H. Harrison's signature on a genuine early-nineteenth-century document, showing the absorbency of the paper, which causes the ink to feather out

40 An enlargement of the letter *H* in the Harrison signature above

Modern inks can only be dated through chemical testing, and their analysis has become very sophisticated. Ink manufacturers, like papermakers, have added compounds so that dates of manufacture can be established. A procedure has also been developed for establishing the amount of time an ink has been on the paper based on the migration of ions into the paper.

As paper ages, it becomes more absorbent, and ink applied to old paper will in most situations be rapidly absorbed into the paper, spreading out in a feathery pattern and creating an outline to the main strokes. The William Henry Harrison signature was forged on a genuine document of the early nineteenth century [39]. The unusual flow of the ink is apparent in this enlargement [40]. (In unusual circumstances, this can occur in genuine writing, but it is generally an immediate indication of forgery.)

The poem supposedly by William Makepeace Thackeray [41], the forged signature of John Quincy Adams [42, 43], and the spurious Anton Rubinstein musical quotation [44, 45] all illustrate the absorption pattern of ink applied many years after the manufacture of the paper.

The forger of the Mormon documents very skillfully prevented this "feathering" from occurring by covering the paper with ammonia hydrochloride or hydrogen peroxide. Two tests did, however, indicate this fake aging.

Sorrows of Werther.

Werther had a love for Charlotte,
   Such as words could never utter,
Would you know how first he met her?
   She was cutting bread and butter.

Charlotte was a married lady,
   And a moral man was Werther,
And for all the wealth of Indies
   Would do nothing that might hurt her.

So he sighed and pined and ogled,
   And his passion boiled & bubbled;
Till he blew his silly brains out,
   And no more was by them troubled.

Charlotte, having seen his body
   Borne before her on a shutter:
Like a well conducted person
   Went on cutting bread & butter.

WM Thackeray

41
A forged poem of William Makepeace Thackeray entitled *Sorrows of Werther* written on old paper, illustrating the "blotter" effect

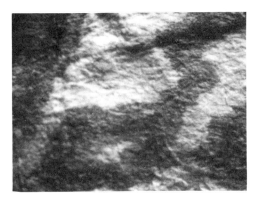

42 A forgery of John Quincy Adams showing the shadow effect of ink recently applied to genuine old paper

43 An enlargement of the letter *a* in the Adams signature

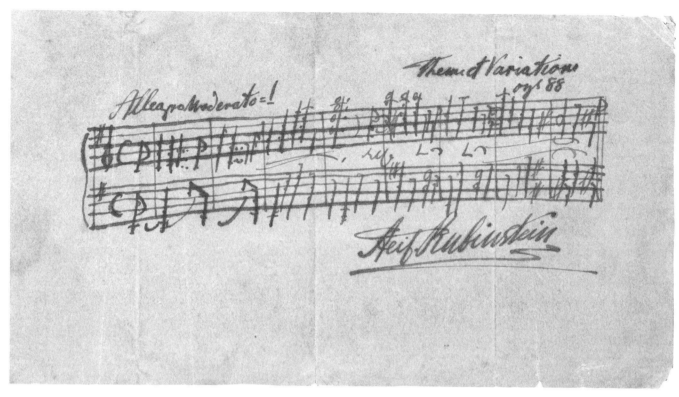

44 A forgery of an Anton Rubinstein musical quotation showing how the ink has feathered when applied to old paper

45 An enlargement of the cross stroke of the letter *t* and the dot from the letter *i* in the above forgery of Rubinstein's signature

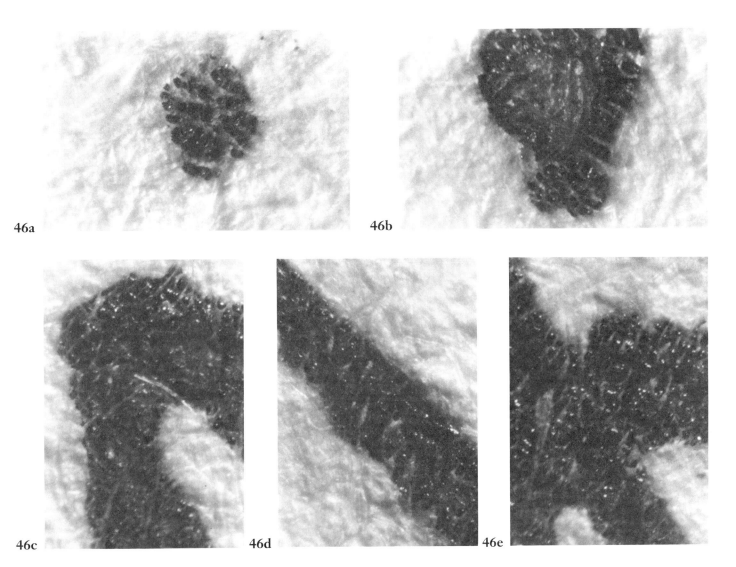

46a

46b

46c

46d

46e

Examination under high-powered ultraviolet light showed a blue fluorescence from the ammonia hydrochloride, immediately giving evidence of chemical treatment. The second effect could only be seen under high magnification and its importance understood only when one realizes that all the letters and documents that fluoresced blue also showed a cracking of the ink — tiny cracks that made each stroke appear like a reptile's skin under high magnification [46a–e]. The ammonia hydrochloride had prevented the feathering pattern of new ink on old paper by raising the pH factor, which caused the ink to coagulate, harden, and crack (pH 7 is the neutral value between acidity or alkalinity; when it is raised, an increase in alkalinity is indicated). A third element was immediately visible to the naked eye in many of Hofmann's forgeries: the chemical used to prevent feathering had caused this ink to run slightly, giving the overall writing a slightly blurred appearance.

46a–e
Enlargements of letters from a forgery by Mark Hofmann, illustrating the results of his attempt to prevent the feathering of ink when applied to old paper. Hofmann had used ammonium hydrochloride to halt the spread of ink, but in doing so, he had also caused the ink to harden and break up into tiny cracks.

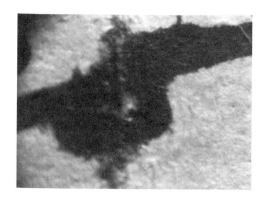

47 An enlargement of the letter *o* from a forged Lincoln letter showing the feathering of the ink caused by writing across an existing fold in the paper

The feathering appearance of new ink on old paper can also occur when ink is applied over an area that has been erased or when a stroke crosses a fold in the paper [47]. The latter is of significance in determining if writing was added after the letter was folded — a common occurrence when a forged portion is added to a genuine document. There will be a broadening and feathering of the stroke as it crosses the fold because the broken paper fibers allow the ink to run to the sides. (The pen may also skip over the ridge of fibers created by the fold.)

When fresh ink crosses a line written at an earlier time, the more recent ink will sometimes, though not always, run out into the pen furrows of the original stroke. However, if the questioned portion of the document was written shortly after the main body of the document, especially if iron gall ink was used, it may be impossible to determine the sequence, particularly if the strokes are shaded and well blotted. In these cases a microscopic examination of the distribution of the fibers is more useful but still may not be entirely conclusive.

WRITING INSTRUMENTS

The traditional quill pen is the most ancient of the writing instruments normally encountered in autograph collecting. The steel pen began to be used in the latter part of the eighteenth century, a fact frequently overlooked by some forgers who, mistakenly believing that quill pens were employed until recent times, have used them on letters written in the earlier part of the twentieth century. The writing of a quill pen differs notably from that of a steel pen, particularly in downstrokes and lateral strokes, which are broadly shaded because of the flexibility of the quill [48]. Additionally, under microscopic examination, the nib marks of steel pens (which

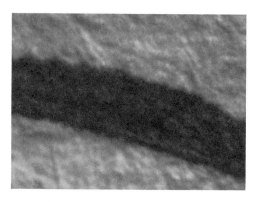

48 An enlargement of a letter written with a quill pen. The quill pen makes no furrows and the writing appears as a smooth stroke.

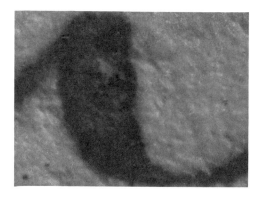

49 An enlargement of a letter written with a steel nib pen showing readily visible nib marks

50 An enlargement of the letter *h* from a forged George Washington letter written with a steel nib pen

create two "furrows" with the ink in between) are clearly visible [49]. Many writers did continue to use the earlier instrument well into the nineteenth century, but the expert should be aware of its decreasing popularity and consequent comparative rarity during the middle and later part of the century.

The presence of nib marks rather than the absence of shaded lateral and downward strokes will instantly unmask many forgeries where a steel pen was used to write what purports to be a pre-1780 letter or document [50]. Frequently these marks are so strong as to be clearly visible to the naked eye. The forger of the George Washington receipt [33] failed to keep enough ink on his pen to cover even superficially his use of a steel pen in a letter where it would have been most unlikely to find a steel pen used.

The ballpoint pen began to be widely used at the end of the Second World War in America and somewhat earlier in Europe. The early examples created very blunt and heavy initial strokes and were prone to skip over the paper fibers without depositing ink. These defects coupled with the poor line quality can give the appearance of being forgeries [51, 52]. In contrast the fiber or felt-tip pen introduced in 1964 created a ribbonlike smooth flow of ink [53].

The use of a defective pen, such as one with a broken nib that spattered or distributed the ink unevenly, usually indicates that the document is genuine. Forgers generally take great care to use perfect materials and to avoid any variation from the normal.

Pencils came into general use about 1785 but were rarely used for letters or documents. Forged pencil writing can be difficult to detect because it can easily be retouched without any indication, and it is not always possible to determine in which direction the stroke was written (the side of the paper fibers where the carbon is deposited can indicate the direction of writing). The propensity for pencil to smudge may indicate that a pocket diary in clear pencil without smudges is suspect, or that a clear and sharp pencil entry among other entries that are slightly smudged was done at a later date. (The pencil writing in the Hitler diaries was clear and fresh, with no smudging. The width of the stroke never varied, indicating it was written with a mechanical pencil, introduced in 1822, which would not have become dull with use.)

51 A genuine complimentary close and signature written by Robert Service with an early ballpoint pen (left)

52 Two enlargements of letters from the Service signature showing ink strokes skipping over the paper fibers without depositing any ink

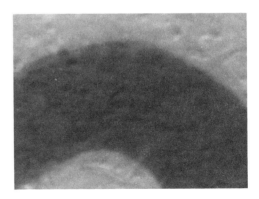

53 An enlargement of a genuine letter from a Lawrence Ferlinghetti letter showing a smooth, wide, and uninterrupted flow of ink, characteristic of a felt-tip pen

POSTAL MARKINGS

Few forgers have given proper consideration to the importance of postal markings, and well-accomplished forgeries can appear to be amateurish attempts when viewed philatelically [54-56]. The first postal hand stamps came into use in England in 1661 and consisted of the month and day printed

54 The integral address leaf of a forged letter of Lord Byron by Major George Byron, showing his con-siderable skill and knowledge in creating an address leaf in keeping with the customs of Byron's time

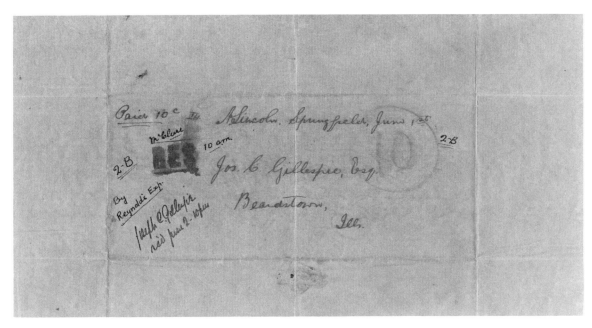

55 The address panel from a forged letter of Abraham Lincoln,
    dated June 2, 1856, illustrating a complete lack of philatelic
    knowledge. Address panels were not marked in this fashion and
    the attempt at a postal stamp does not approximate any used.

56 The address leaf from a forged letter of Sir Walter Scott by
    Antique Smith showing the correct postal markings that would
    be found on an address sheet at this time

in a small circle; in 1695 a straight-line postmark bearing the name of the post town was introduced. Germany adopted this practice of incorporating the name of the town in 1720. Italy followed in 1740, and the United States in the late 1750s. Adhesive postage stamps were first used in England in May 1840 and in the United States seven years later (although private mailing companies employed their own adhesive stamps commencing in 1842, and the postmasters in New York, Providence, and St. Louis issued their own adhesive postage stamps in 1845). A comprehensive postal history guide will approximately date both the postal markings and postage stamps independent of the purported date on the letter.

The Mormon forger, Hofmann, had a knowledge of philately and consequently forged some letters by obtaining an unimportant letter of the correct period written on one page with the integral address and postmarked leaf attached. The leaf with the letter was detached and discarded and the forgery written on the verso of the correctly postmarked address leaf (this did, however, leave the problem of the address panel being written in a different hand than the purported letter on the verso).

Before 1845, letters were normally folded to utilize the center of the final leaf as the address panel, and the folded letter was then sealed with wax for transmittal. Envelopes are rarely encountered prior to this date, although they became quite popular once they were introduced and rapidly replaced the older method. Before the introduction of the envelope, a separate piece of paper was sometimes, though infrequently, folded around the letter to cover it for mailing.

FACSIMILES

The overwhelming majority of facsimiles (which are in fact engraved, lithographed, or printed reproductions of handwriting) are readily apparent under low magnification (10X, the maximum size of an easily used magnifying glass). The most noticeable characteristics are the flat, even appearance of the ink with no variation in flow and areas within the pen stroke which are not inked. (The same effect can result in a genuine piece if the paper fibers are depressed in a spot and the pen skips over the area, leaving it untouched; in most facsimiles these uninked spots occur throughout the writing, not just in one isolated area.) Some facsimiles are, especially if lithographed, very deceptive. Among the most difficult to detect and the most frequently offered as genuine are military documents bearing Adolf Hitler's lithographed signature and letters thanking his unnamed correspondent for birthday or Christmas greetings [57-62].

57 A genuine signature of Adolf Hitler

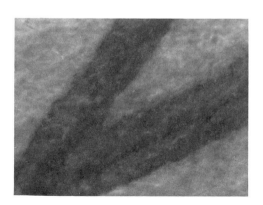

58 An enlargement of a letter from the above genuine signature

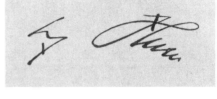

61 A facsimile signature from the
Hitler document [60]

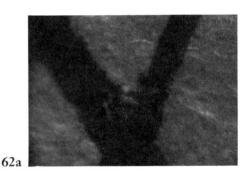

62a

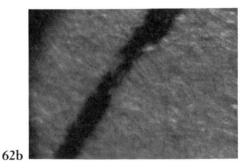

62b

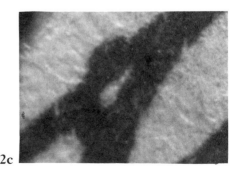

62c

60 A partly printed document dated December 19, 1941,
with a facsimile signature of the Führer

62a–c Three enlargements of letters
from the facsimile signature

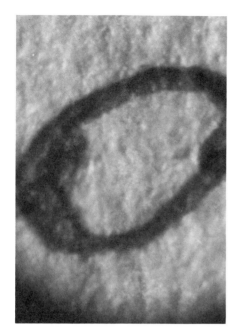

64 An enlargement from a genuine letter written by George V showing a smooth flow of ink

Many facsimiles are also of a nature that should make an examiner suspicious. Purported handwritten letters without a specific salutation sending thanks for birthday or Christmas greetings, or written just after an important event, such as an election or award (when the writer would receive a large number of letters), automatically should be suspect. It should seem unlikely to all but the most gullible that George V could have sent a personal message to every soldier who served in the First World War [63-65], or that Churchill could have personally written to all those who commiserated with him over the loss of the election in 1945 or those who wrote each year congratulating him on his birthday [66-68]. Additional examples of facsimiles are illustrated in figures 69 through 75.

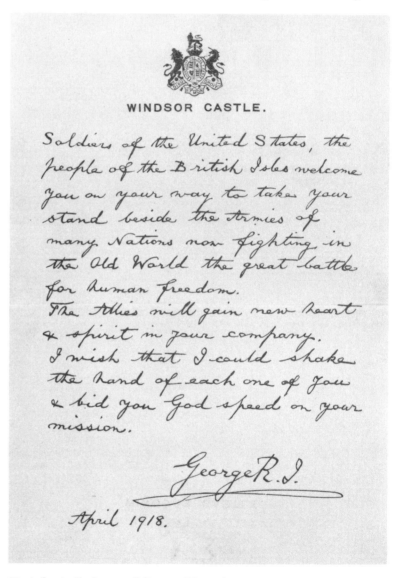

WINDSOR CASTLE.

Soldiers of the United States, the people of the British Isles welcome you on your way to take your stand beside the Armies of many Nations now fighting in the Old World the great battle for human freedom.
The Allies will gain new heart & spirit in your company.
I wish that I could shake the hand of each one of you & bid you God speed on your mission.

George R.I.

April 1918.

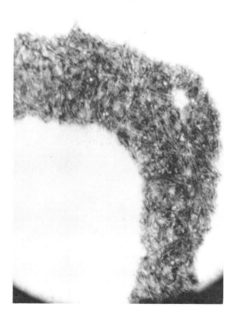

65 An enlargement from the facsimile letter of George V [63] showing an ink void

63 A facsimile letter of George V sending a personal message to soldiers who served in World War I

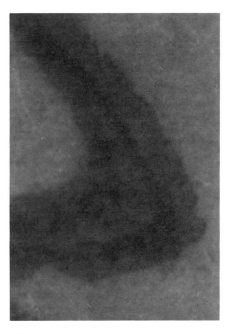

67 An enlargement from a genuine letter by Churchill showing a smooth flow of ink

28, HYDE PARK GATE,

LONDON, S.W.7.

Thank you so much for your good wishes on my birthday,

Winston S. Churchill

November 30 ⸿ 60

66 A facsimile letter of Winston Churchill acknowledging birthday wishes sent to him

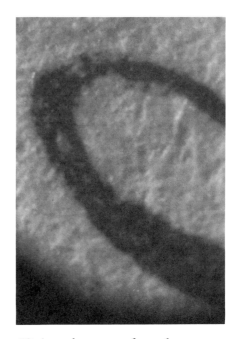

68 An enlargement from the Churchill facsimile letter [66] showing ink voids

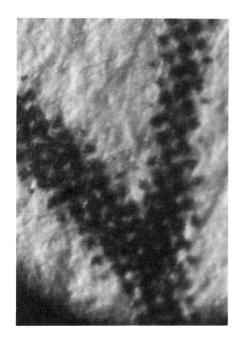

70 An enlargement of a letter from the de Gaulle thank you letter [69]

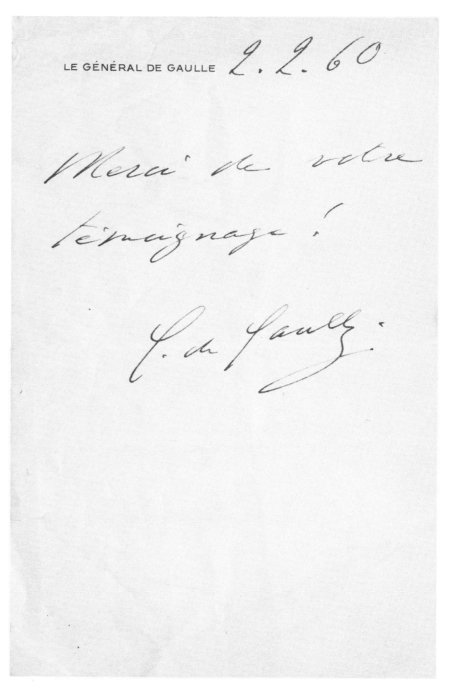

LE GÉNÉRAL DE GAULLE

69 A facsimile letter of Charles de Gaulle sending thanks

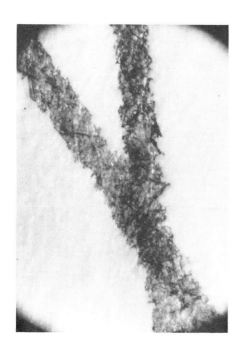

71 An enlargement of a letter from a genuine de Gaulle letter

Four score and seven years ago our fathers brought forth upon this continent, a new nation, conceived in Liberty, and dedicated to the proposition that all men are created equal.

Now we are engaged in a great civil war, testing whether that nation, or any nation so conceived, and so dedicated, can long endure. We are met on a great battle field of that war. We have come to dedicate a portion of that field, as a final resting place for those who here gave their lives, that that nation might live. It is altogether fitting and proper that we should do this.

But, in a larger sense, we can not dedicate— we can not consecrate— we can not hallow— this ground. The brave men, living and dead, who struggled here, have consecrated it, far above our poor power to add or detract. The world will little note, nor long remember, what we say here, but it can never forget what they did here. It is for us, the living, rather, to be dedicated here to the unfinished work which they who fought here, have, thus far, so nobly advanced. It is rather for us to be here dedicated to the great task remaining before

72 A facsimile of a speech of Abraham Lincoln

73 An enlargement of a letter from the Lincoln speech [72]

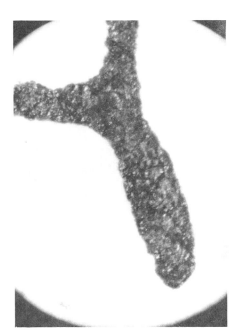

74 An enlargement of a letter from a genuine Lincoln letter

41

75a-g Facsimile signatures and enlargements of letters from the signatures
showing areas that are void of ink

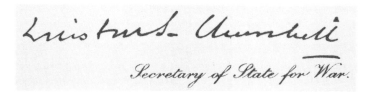

75a Winston S. Churchill

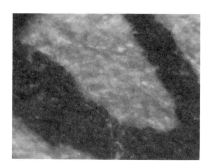

75b Queen Victoria

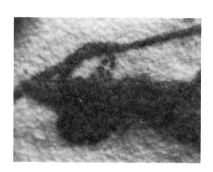

75c Lord Byron

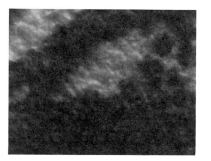

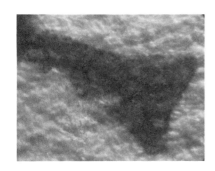

Very sincerely yours,

Franklin D. Roosevelt

hard,

75d Franklin D. Roosevelt

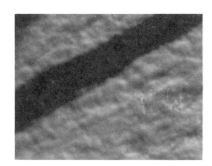

Sincerely yours,

Harry Truman

75e Harry S Truman

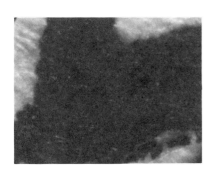

with best wishes

Dwight D. Eisenhower

75f Dwight D. Eisenhower

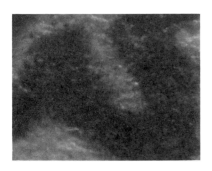

; and I am, in the meantime,
yours very truly
Robert Louis Stevenson

75g Robert Louis Stevenson

3
Comparisons of Handwriting and Typewriting

Comparisons between one handwriting known to be genuine and another that is questioned are frequently made. A dealer in historical documents is as likely to undertake such comparisons to determine if the questioned writing is by the famous person rather than a contemporary of the same name as he is to determine if it is a forgery. At any time in history there may be people living in the same area with the same name. All of these persons are likely to have gone to similar schools and learned basically the same methods of handwriting.

When a dealer encounters a letter supposedly written early in the career of a well-known person, the handwriting is usually quite different from that with which he or she is familiar. The only course is to compare it with other letters of the same date known to be genuine (frequently from examples in an archive containing the person's papers).

Whether the expert is pursuing a possible mistaken identity or a forgery, the methods are the same. Examples of handwriting independently known to be genuine must be obtained, and most important of all, these examples must be from the same time period as the questioned material and written under the same circumstances. A speech, for example, is normally written much larger and more legibly than notes taken down at a meeting. If two examples as different in origin as these were compared, the results could be inaccurate. A signature on an important document should not be compared to one on a routine document such as a check because people always have a tendency to sign an important or formal document much more carefully. Many people's handwriting changes over a period of years, while others' handwriting remains unchanged. Moreover, some, for example, Thackeray and Masefield, had two distinct styles of handwriting that they used interchangeably [76]. All of these factors must be considered in order to arrive at an accurate conclusion.

The possibility that a letter was written by a parent rather than a son or daughter must be considered; or, as

reading too - lonely in this great town (The towns are great but the Society in them very small, and as well defined as Society in European towns) He thought so well of me that I was quite frightened, and felt a Domine how sum dignus - Bon dieu how I should like to be as good as that friendly soul thinks me to be! He gave me Emersons Essays Vol I had never read. Have you? They are very wise and benevolent. They come to very like conclusions to those wh the Worldling who writes these presents to you reaches sometimes - and as I read honest Emerson, I fancy I have known it all before. I wrote from Philadelphia didn't I? I found very good and true friends there too - by heaven they are very tender hearted & friendly I wonder why they should be so good to me?(the fountain pen I think is already beginning to fail, don't you?)(Since the above was written the fountain pen has gone off with a spirt

but it is something like the old gold pen, and will do for drawing and dipping into the ink like ordinary pen wont it? - It would be good sport and practise to stop here for a month and draw negroes. negroes and horses - negroes and mules - Negro boys - old women &c. They are endless

76 A letter written by William Makepeace Thackeray
in his slanting and vertical hands, January 27, [1856]

45

with Wordsworth, his wife. Handwriting characteristics pass from father to son and mother to daughter with quite striking similarity. The expert must be aware if the person in question had a child sharing the same name who may have written the questioned letter.

Examples of genuine handwriting can frequently be found in the many excellent volumes of facsimiles that are listed in the bibliography of this book. If not found there, the best approach is to contact a library likely to have original examples of the person's handwriting and to obtain photocopies for the purpose of comparison. Library directories or biographies are the best sources for locations of a person's papers.

The most useful and accurate method of comparing two handwritings is, literally, side by side. After examining the general flow of handwriting in the two examples and looking for any obvious idiosyncracies, such as the significant downward slant at the end of each of Hitler's lines of writing, all similar letter patterns need to be assembled horizontally [77, 78]. Figures 77 and 78 demonstrate various letters of the alphabet taken from the few known letters and manuscripts in Hitler's handwriting. In this case, the questioned letters and combinations are the actual ones taken from the Hitler

77 Words beginning with the capital letter *P* from the Hitler diaries, forged by Kujau

diaries. This analysis was not necessary to show that the Hitler diaries bore little resemblance to Hitler's genuine handwriting, but it was necessary to convince editors that they had been wrong in believing other authentication reports.

There are a number of handwriting characteristics that are common to many writers and should *not* be given great weight when making comparisons: dots of the *i* and crossing of the *t* made far to the right; the loop on the lower case *e*, *a*, and *o* left open; dots of the *i* in the form of short strokes; pen raises after *v*, *w*, and *b*; and the habit of decreasing the size of characters toward the conclusion of a word.

The general layout of a letter — the location of the date line, salutation, and closing; the indentions for paragraphs and the width of margins; the spacing between lines, words, characters, and paragraphs and between capitals and small letters in the same words — should be analyzed and compared. Other aspects to consider are the relation of letters, words, and paragraphs to a theoretical baseline, the location of punctuation marks in relation to the theoretical baseline and to the words they precede or follow, the general attention of the writer, the care in writing, and the care in following the outline of the letter. Terminology is very important; if all examples but the questioned one use the same closing or salutation, this should be cause for concern.

The connections between letters are often telling characteristics. There should be consistent variations before and after particular letters; the connections between all letters should be studied for angular or curved connections, pen lifts, and spaces; and the pattern of connections between particular letters should be noted. The fineness or bluntness of beginning and ending strokes should be considered, as should the length, slant, and shape of beginning and ending strokes and the distance that upward strokes are traced back at sharp angles in connections at the tops of letters. A measurement of the length, width, and slant of the upper-loop letters *b*, *f*, *h*, *k*, and *l* should be compared with the lower-loop letters *g*, *j*, *y*, and *z*. The formation of certain letters should be looked at carefully, especially that of *a*, *r*, and *w* as final letters; *o*, *s*, and *t* as both initial and final letters; the initial and intermediate *c*; the capital *E*; the words *of* and *the*; and any particular letter groups and forms the writer may have an unusual method of executing. One should note the slant of the letter *s* and its angularity, curvature, roundness, size, shading, slant, and proportions; and the formation of the same letter twice, for example, *ee*, *ff*, *dd*, and *ll*. Capitals also provide many possibilities for individual characteristics.

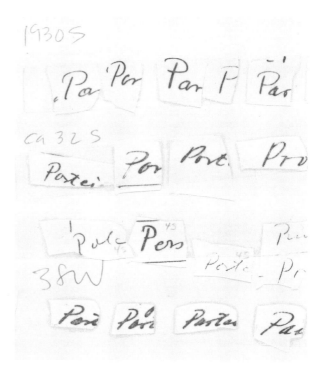

78 This assembly of words beginning with the capital letter *P*, written by Adolf Hitler in the 1930s, reveals differences in letter patterns when compared with Konrad Kujau's forged writing [77].

Next, the expert should examine the movement of the pen and the pressure applied by observing the smoothness or roughness and the apparent speed of writing in upward and downward strokes. Pressure on the pen will be indicated by the width of the line and depth of indentation and by variations in pen pressure in upward, downward, and horizontal strokes. Unevenness of pressure on the pen may be indicated by comparative smoothness or roughness of the right or left side of the pen stroke, but a writer's habit of applying more pressure to one side of the pen can be properly evaluated only when comparing characters written on similar paper with similar ink.

The shading of the pen strokes may provide valuable clues. The frequency of shading on each upward and downward stroke should be reviewed, as should the smoothness or roughness of shading and the vertical or horizontal shading (which depends on the position of the pen in the hand).

Still other characteristics to be considered are the slant of the writing, including the slant of the upward and downward strokes, the angle of the slant of all vertical characters, and the angle of the slant in the last part of the letters *b*, *m*, *n*, and *p*. The proportions of individual letters in relation to each other and the ligatures between, as well as any characters that are consistently and significantly too large or too small in relation to other characters, must be studied.

Characters that are in a print hand rather than written provide a special set of problems, and differing characteristics from script must be examined. These include the "incorrect" formation of *a*, *g*, *r*, *m*, *n*, and *p*; the number of pen lifts to make each character; the direction of strokes; the general shading, slant, proportion, width, and height of characters; the alignment at the top and bottom of each character; any letters consistently written larger or smaller than the normal size; the spacing between lines, letters, words, and paragraphs; the angularity of the strokes in *A*, *K*, *M*, *N*, *V*, *W*, *X*, *Y*, and *Z*; the curvature in the left side of *C*, *G*, *O*, and *Q* and in the right side of *B*, *D*, *P*, and *R*; the finishing strokes of *G*, *K*, and *R*; the proportions in *E*, *F*, and *L*; and, if all the letters are capitals, the relative size of each initial letter in each word, sentence, or paragraph relative to the following letters.

TYPEWRITING COMPARISONS

Typewriting is most frequently examined to identify the earliest date that the typeface could have been used and to identify its country of origin. The first practical typewriter

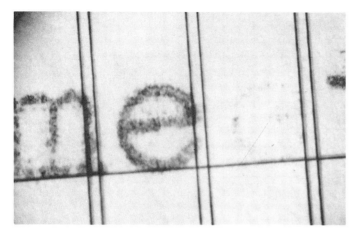

79 The character *e* reveals a type defect in spacing.

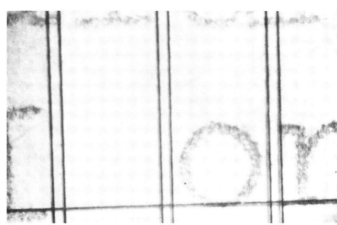

80 The character *l* is aligned below the baseline.

81 The vertical slant of the character *r* is not at ninety
degrees in relation to the baseline.

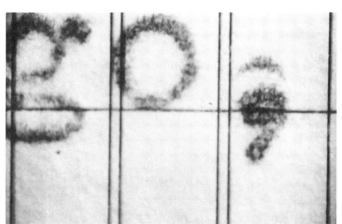

82 The offset pressure causes a shadow of the comma to
appear above it.

was developed by Christopher Latham Sholes in 1867, and
after improvements were made, it was marketed by Remington
and Sons of Ilion, New York, in 1874. Examples of typefaces
are easily obtained, and it is a relatively simple task to match
the questioned example and establish its date and country
of manufacture. A typewritten quotation signed by Albert
Einstein, prepared on an IBM Selectric, which was invented
six years after his death, is obviously highly suspicious! Comparisons between examples of typewriting are made when it
is suspected that typewritten letters or manuscripts supposedly written by different persons may have been prepared on
the same typewriter, indicating the substantial probability of
forgery. A series of false letters on genuine Third Reich
stationery was uncovered when it was shown that while a
German typewriter of the period was used, it would not have
been likely that all of the Nazi leaders had their letters done
on the same typewriter.

Fortunately, comparisons of typewriting before 1961 are usually definitive in their conclusions, and the criteria are fewer than in handwriting comparisons. Initial examination should reveal any unusual breaks in particular characters or defects in spacing. In the absence of such unique features, typewriting templates are used to compare the design, size, and proportion of the characters and particularly the alignment of the characters in relation to each other and to the baseline. It is also important to measure the vertical and horizontal slant of the characters and, if necessary, the pressure of the strike of the typewriter key — that is, the amount of pressure on each side of the character [79-82].

The introduction of the IBM Selectric typewriter in 1961, like the introduction of the autopen machines (see chapter 6) some years earlier, revolutionized the field of questioned typewriting examination. It is virtually impossible to distinguish between examples of IBM Selectric typewriters using the same typefaces unless there has been damage to one of the balls. The uniformity that the type ball creates, while a boon to better-quality typing, has posed very significant problems for those attempting to identify specific typewriters. The question of modern typewriters has become so difficult and technical that a number of questioned document examiners specialize only in this very narrow area.

Typewriting is also studied to determine if there has been normal wear on a typeface supposedly used over a period of time. The labels of the Hitler diaries, for example, were all prepared on a typewriter manufactured before 1932, and the same typewriter was used for all of the labels through 1945. This practice may seem quite normal, but a very careful examination of the typewriter impressions revealed that the typefaces had not shown the wear from year to year they would have had they had normal use.

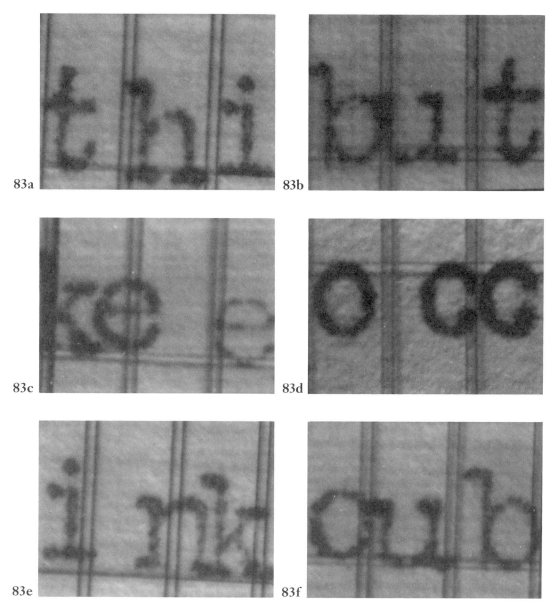

83a-f Typical idiosyncracies of mechanical typewriters

4

Famous Forgers:
Their Successes and Downfalls

The Ptolemaic rulers of ancient Egypt were among the earliest patrons of literary forgers, offering substantial sums for manuscripts bearing the names of the leading writers of ancient Greece. James A. Farrer in his classic work, *Literary Forgeries*, states that forgers flourished in Greece long before the Christian era. He discusses in detail the numerous literary hoaxes from ancient times to the nineteenth century and points out that prior to the nineteenth century forgers, including the most noted, were chiefly concerned with the intellectual forging of literary works and paid little attention to the details of handwriting and materials.

Today, it seems inconceivable that such forgeries could ever have been considered genuine. However, systematic and detailed document examinations were virtually unknown, and forgers were able to work almost without hindrance. These early forgeries rarely appear in today's market, much to the delight of those collectors who specialize in fakes. The stories of these early forgers are an interesting sidelight to the history of autograph collecting.

The young eighteenth-century English poet, Thomas Chatterton, invented a fifteenth-century monk whom he named Rowley and attributed his own poetry to this fictitious character, believing that his genuine literary creations would not be accepted without the mantle of antiquity. The poems were written in an antique hand on parchment, and the young Chatterton intended to reveal his hoax once the poetry was acclaimed and accepted by the literary critics of his day. His deception died in its infancy when Horace Walpole, to whom he had appealed for aid in publishing the poems, consulted several experts, with the result that the manuscripts were quickly denounced as forgeries. Chatterton, only seventeen years old, committed suicide — a great tragedy, for his poetic talent was considerable. Samuel Taylor Coleridge, John Keats, and Dante Gabriel Rossetti wrote poems lamenting his death, and Chatterton's forged manuscripts are very rare and sought after.

William Henry Ireland, in contrast, was remarkably successful with his forgeries of Shakespearean documents. He was the son of Samuel Ireland, an engraver whose love of Shakespeare and ambition to own a Shakespeare letter inspired his son to begin his career as a forger. Ireland produced volumes purported to be from Shakespeare's library with annotations by the Bard of Avon, drawings by him, a love poem to Ann Hathaway, correspondence between Shakespeare and his patron Southampton, and letters written to Shakespeare. The incredible acceptance of his literary creations encouraged Ireland to produce fragments of the manuscripts of *Hamlet* and *King Lear* and finally to create a new drama attributed to Shakespeare, entitled *Vortigern and Rowena*. This work proved to be his undoing. Richard Brinsley Sheridan contracted to produce it at Drury Lane with John Philip Kemble in the lead, but Sheridan's disenchantment with the play increased as Ireland slowly produced each section of the manuscript. Sheridan finally refused to advertise the play as Shakespeare's and rejected Ireland's offered compromise that it be advertised as a tragedy "discovered among the Shakespearean manuscripts in the possession of Mr. Ireland."

Kemble went considerably further, presenting on the same bill with *Vortigern and Rowena* a musical farce, *My Grandmother*, which involved the gullibility of an art collector. He also expressed the intention of presenting the premiere of the play on April Fool's Day but was frustrated in this; the first production occurred on April 2, 1796. Two days before, Edmond Malone had published his *Inquiry into the Authenticity of Certain Miscellaneous Papers*, which attacked the literary qualities of the fraudulent drama and led to Ireland's downfall. The interest in his forgeries gave rise to nineteenth-century forgers who specialized in forging Ireland's forgeries [84]. Today, original Ireland forgeries, despite their almost quaint amateurish quality, are highly sought after.

In the later nineteenth century, the exceptionally skillful forger, Major George Gordon De Luna Byron (also known as Monsieur Memoir and De Gibler), represented himself as the illegitimate son of Lord Byron, and his close physical resemblance lent credence to his claim. He lived in the United States but offered his forgeries in his native England and was very accomplished in forging the writing of his "father" [85] and his "father's" contemporaries, Keats and Shelley. His adeptness in forging postmarks and seals, as well as the handwriting, paper, and ink, was unsurpassed at the time; his forgeries are today uncovered only through very careful examination. His abilities were reflected in the fact that he was able to sell his forged Byron letters to Byron's own

84 A forged manuscript of William Shakespeare
by William Henry Ireland

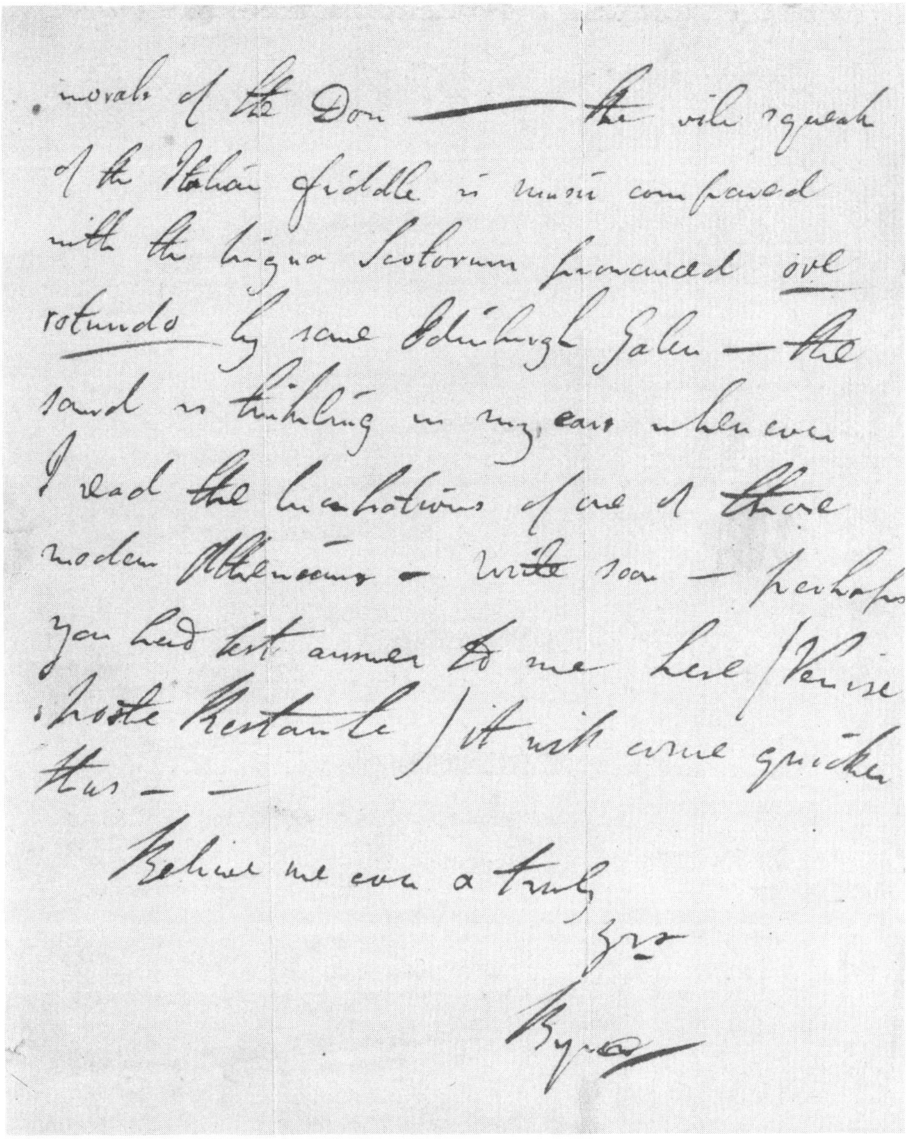
morals of the Don —— the vile squeak of the Italian fiddle is music compared with the lingua Scotorum pronounced ore rotundo by some Edinburgh Galen — the sound is tinkling in my ears whenever I read the lucubrations of one of those modern Athenians — write soon — perhaps you had best answer to me here (Venise Poste Restante) it will come quicker thus — —

Believe me ever & truly

yrs

Byron

85 A forged letter of Lord Byron by Major George Gordon Byron

publisher, who presumably had seen a substantial number of genuine letters with which he could have compared them. The detection of his fabrications occurred with a series of Shelley letters in which he plagiarized an obscure magazine article. Tennyson happened to show a copy of the letters to the son of the author of the original article, who was immediately able to reveal the source of the text of the letters, thus leading to the discovery of Byron as a major forger.

"Antique" Smith, as Alexander H. Smith became known, was a highly skilled forger whose fabrications can cause problems for today's collector. His career began in Edinburgh, Scotland, in the 1880s; with great adroitness (though in many cases his forgeries are very carelessly executed) he forged letters and manuscripts attributed to Robert Burns [86],

86 A forgery of Robert Burns's poem, *An Elegy on the death of Roobert Romsseaux, a poor Poet,* by Alexander "Antique" Smith

Sir Walter Scott [87], Mary Queen of Scots, Oliver Cromwell, Edmund Burke, William Pitt, William Makepeace Thackeray, James I of England, Charles I and II of England, and others. His calligraphy was frequently excellent and was accomplished without tracing. His forgeries have acquired a genuine appearance of age, and they are occasionally offered for sale in England and the United States. Smith was arrested in 1892 and found guilty of forging 162 letters and manuscripts (see also pp. 83-89).

The Frenchman Denis Vrain-Lucas perpetrated the most outlandish forgery hoax of the nineteenth-century forgers. Beginning in 1861, he sold to Michael Chasles, a noted French mathematician, a collection of forgeries that over the years totaled 27,000 letters, manuscripts, and documents. No skill was involved in his forgeries, and his success was based upon his ability to gain the confidence of the gullible Chasles. Among the autographs sold by Vrain-Lucas (all of which were written in modern French) were love letters between Cleopatra and Caesar and letters by Judas Iscariot, Mary Magdalene, Pontius Pilate, Lazarus (before and after his resurrection), Joan of Arc, Attila the Hun, Alexander the Great, Herod, Cicero, Pomperry, Sappho, and Dante. This fantastic under-

88 A forged letter of George Washington, dated February 12, 1781, by Robert Spring

taking was the subject of an interesting pamphlet written by the mid-nineteenth-century French dealer and autograph expert Etienne Charavay. The furor that led to Vrain-Lucas's exposure occurred when he forged a letter of Blaise Pascal to Robert Boyle, in which the former claimed that he, rather than Newton, had discovered the law of universal gravitation. The date Vrain-Lucas supplied for the letter would have made Newton only ten years old at the time of its writing, and his fabrications were thereby exposed.

Robert Spring has the questionable distinction of being the first significant forger in the United States. His infamous career began in the 1850s. He is noted principally for his numerous forgeries of payment orders by George Washington, initially written on genuine printed forms of the Office of Discount and Deposit at Baltimore and later, when his supplies of these forms were exhausted, written completely in Washington's forged handwriting. His forgeries of Benjamin Franklin payment orders are equally excellent, although not as numerous. All of Spring's work is characterized by a lack of hesitation, relative speed, and confidence [88]. A careful study of his forgeries will reveal common characteristics, and the handwriting expert soon becomes adept at identifying his work (see also pp. 77-82).

While Spring was the first major forger in the United States, Joseph Cosey was undoubtedly the most prolific. Cosey devoted considerable time and care to the paper, ink, handwriting characteristics, and habits of particular periods. His forgeries can therefore cause considerable difficulty for modern collectors. Cosey's career began with his discovery of a batch of unused Monnier's 1856 watermarked paper of the same blue shade that Abraham Lincoln favored for his legal documents, and he undertook a series of legal briefs in the forged handwriting of Lincoln. These were followed by endorsements on genuine letters of a type Lincoln frequently did endorse. Cosey studied the types and colors of paper favored by various persons and dyed his own stock of antique papers to match those normally employed by the persons whose writing he was forging. The persons he specialized in are John Adams, Samuel Adams, Francis Bacon, Aaron Burr, Samuel L. Clemens, Mary Baker Eddy [89], Button Gwinnett, Patrick Henry, Richard Henry Lee, Mary Todd Lincoln, Thomas Lynch, John Marshall [90], and Edgar Allan Poe. Cosey's forgeries, like those of Spring, fortunately have their own characteristics that the expert learns to identify (see also pp. 69-77).

89 A forged letter of Mary Baker Eddy, addressed to Sarah Dean, by Joseph Cosey

Washington, Feb. 7.th 1804

My dear Sir,

I am writing you these few lines to express my pleasure at the result of your work as foreman of the jury in Col.o Taylor's case. You were fortunate in having as an aid the invoices of Mr. Bassett, a man of character & intelligence. My own opinion was and is that on legal principles Col.o Taylor's testimony was admissible. They rejected it however, and the matter stood. The whole case was a curious impeachment. The present doctrine seems to be that a judge giving a legal opinion contrary to the opinion of the legislature is liable to impeachment.

I shall be in Richmond again early next week and shall take a run over and see Col.o Taylor if he is at home.

You have no doubt heard of the death of Mr. Nelson.

With much respect esteem I am, my dear Sir, your obt.

J Marshall

Col.o Gamble
Richmond.

90 A forged letter of John Marshall, dated February 7, 1804, by Joseph Cosey

Charles Weisberg, also an American, was active primarily in the 1930s. While not as prolific as Cosey, his creations were more skillfully accomplished. Land surveys of George Washington were his specialty; but he also forged letters and manuscripts of Heinrich Heine, Walt Whitman, and Abraham Lincoln [91]. Coincidentally, his Lincoln forgeries are similar to those of Cosey and are principally endorsements written adjacent to the text of the letter to which Lincoln was replying, rather than on the reverse, which was Lincoln's custom. His nefarious activities led to his imprisonment during the 1940s, and he died in prison in 1945.

91 A forged letter of George Washington, dated May 16, 1785, by Charles Weisberg

Eugene Field, who wrote the well-known poem *Little Boy Blue*, was one of America's beloved poets at the turn of the twentieth century. His son, Eugene Field II, did not inherit his literary skills but did inherit, as many children do, a very similar writing style. Field II, after his father's death in 1895, made an income from selling his father's manuscripts and books from his library and like some before him, decided to create new material signed by the poet when the cupboard was bare [92-94].

At the beginning, Field II forged only books signed by his father and then his father's poems, but he was soon encouraged by his success to add forgeries of more valuable literary autographs to his repertoire. Samuel L. Clemens was his favorite, and the example with Field's authentication on the verso [22, 26] is typical of his work. The Frederic Remington forgery incorporating the drawing of a bucking horse has also been attributed to Field [24].

Any Clemens material bearing an authentication by Field is automatically suspect, as are any Remington signatures such as those illustrated. All poems by Eugene Field must also be closely examined to determine precisely which Field wrote them.

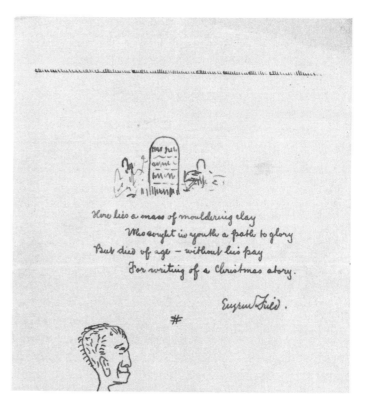

92 A forgery of Eugene Field's poem, *A Bad Imitation of Good Dr. Watts*, by his son, Eugene Field II

93 A forged poem of Eugene Field with sketches, by Eugene Field II

94
A forgery of Eugene Field's poem, entitled *A Proper Sonet* and illustrated with sketches, by Eugene Field II

An unnamed employee of a major French library created one of the most accomplished archival forgeries in the mid-1960s. This archive supposedly composed a part of the personal papers of Hector Berlioz, and the forger knew exactly what would have been found in such an archive. This forger's skill was not in imitating Berlioz's handwriting but in creating the archive — everything from rent receipts made out to Berlioz and incoming letters from unknown persons to contemporary newspapers and printed sheet music from the most minor as well as the most major composers, all inscribed to Berlioz. Never before had anyone created such a complete archive, with hundreds of pieces of little commercial value but all creating the impression that the forger did indeed have a group of Berlioz's own papers. To these hundreds of worthless letters and documents he then added dozens of letters of Berlioz, from the very routine to the most important.

95
A forged letter of Hector Berlioz by an employee of a major French library who created an entire Berlioz archive

> Some say the world will end in fire,
> Some say in ice.
> From what I've tasted of desire,
> I hold with those who favor fire
> But if it had to perish twice,
> I think I know enough of hate
> To say that for destruction ice
> Is also great
> And would suffice.
>
> Robert Frost

FORGERY

96 A forgery of Robert Frost's poem, *Fire and Ice*, by Thomas McNamara

The content of the important Berlioz letters almost immediately unmasked this clever hoax when two English dealers specializing in music, Richard MacNutt and Albi Rosenthal, were discussing how Berlioz could have held the musical views expressed in the letters, realized that he could not have, and then proceeded to examine the letters more closely. The forger admitted his hoax, and virtually all of the letters were retrieved and destroyed. The example illustrated on the previous page is the only one I know to be extant [95].

The Robert Frost manuscript illustrated above is one of dozens that were forged and sold by Thomas McNamara, a highly skilled forger who sold many of his forged Frost poems

To Thomas Francis:

      I make really very little money.

      What of it ?

      I prefer the grass with the rain on it

        the short grass before my headlights

      when I am turning the car—

      a degenerate trait, no doubt.

      It would ruin England.

      It certainly would!

William Carlos Williams
9 Ridge Road
Rutherford, New Jersey

William Carlos Williams

to antique dealers, each matted and framed with a contemporary photograph [96]. McNamara, a former curator of the George H. Browne collection of Robert Frost at Plymouth State College in New Hampshire, also forged signed typescripts of William Carlos Williams [97] and similar typescripts by Langston Hughes. His attempts to forge other authors were far less accomplished. Any Robert Frost poem not inscribed to a specific person in the lower left should be carefully scrutinized, as should any typescripts by Williams or Hughes. McNamara was sentenced to one year in a federal prison in 1978, eight years after he began his career.

97 A forged typescript of William Carlos Williams by Thomas McNamara

Another modern forger had a much briefer career. Various dealers have determined that an aide to a congressman who reputedly had close ties to the Kennedy family forged and sold a number of John F. Kennedy fakes, including a copy of Kennedy's most famous quotation, "Ask not what your coun-

THE WHITE HOUSE
WASHINGTON

Jan. 20th 1961.

And so, my fellow Americans—ask not what your country can do for you—ask what you can do for your country—

Jack Kennedy

Washington D.C.

98 A forgery of John F. Kennedy's most famous quotation

try can do for you, but what you can do for your country" [98]. This was written on genuine White House stationery, but the paper was watermarked 1981. Because of the alleged forger's connection with the Kennedy family he was initially successful in selling a number of pieces, but within a matter of weeks dealers realized that the handwriting did not match genuine examples and the alleged forger bought back all of his creations.

Most modern forgers have generally limited themselves to forging signatures on otherwise genuine items, such as souvenir postage stamp sheets (Adolf Hitler), photographs, and other pieces where the age of the paper is not a factor that will betray them and the ink would be relatively modern.

A very insidious type of forgery has emerged in recent years and has been offered by several honest and reliable dealers. These are genuine signatures with forged statements added to the paper after they were signed. There have been many versions of Richard Nixon's letter of resignation offered on the market without any statement that the signature on the so-called letter was actually signed on the flyleaf of a book or on a blank page by someone who had approached Nixon in person. The flyleaf was later removed from the book and the letter of resignation typed above the signature. This has been done with a number of modern personalities, and dealers offering them are as deceitful as any forger if they do not correctly catalog what they are selling as a signature to which has been added the important text.

These textual forgeries have not been limited to politicians; I once ordered what was described as a *Typewritten Quotation Signed* of Douglas MacArthur, "Old soldiers never die, they just fade away," together with a quotation signed by Albert Einstein, "$E = mc^2$." When I received the two pieces I realized that while the two signatures were certainly genuine the quotations were done on a typewriter of the same make. In returning the pieces to the dealer I added a note saying that while I had great respect for Einstein, I had no idea that he had invented the IBM Selectric eight years before IBM had! The dealer telephoned to ask what I was referring to, and I pointed out that both pieces were typed on an IBM Selectric, using in fact the same typeface that the dealer used to type his invoice.

The century's two most important forgers — Konrad Kujau, forger of the Hitler diaries, and Mark Hofmann, forger of the Mormon documents — will be discussed at length in chapters 7 and 8.

5

An Analysis of Major Forgeries

This chapter is an examination of four excellent forgeries: a Benjamin Franklin document and an Abraham Lincoln letter by Joseph Cosey, a George Washington letter by Robert Spring, and a Robert Burns letter by Antique Smith. All four are very well executed fabrications, and similar examples by these forgers have been passed as genuine on numerous occasions. However, when compared with genuine examples in an analytic manner, the differences become immediately apparent.

99 A genuine payment authorization signed by Benjamin Franklin

BENJAMIN FRANKLIN

Documents such as the payment authorization signed by Benjamin Franklin are among the most common forms of Franklin documents encountered [99]. They are also those that are most commonly forged [100].

Documents are easier to forge than handwritten letters, but there are still many factors to examine, as illustrated here. Cosey has forged Franklin's signature excellently, making very few errors. However, he made no attempt to imitate the signature of John Nicholson, an important financier of the time; nor did he pay any attention to the signature of David Rittenhouse, another well-known leader of the time [101-106].

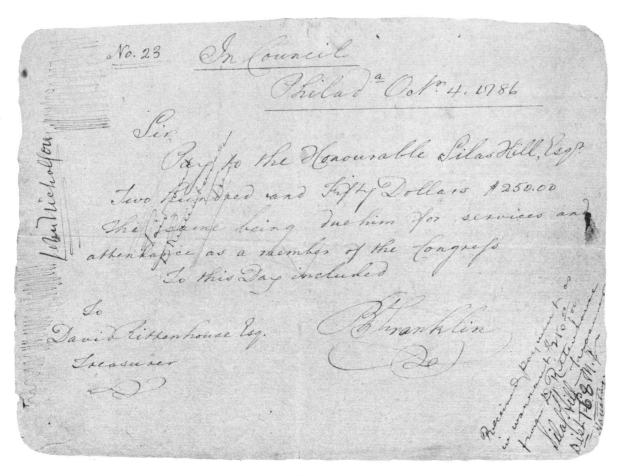

100 A forged payment authorization by Joseph Cosey

101 A genuine signature of Benjamin Franklin

102 A forged Franklin signature by Joseph Cosey

103 A genuine signature of John Nicholson

104 A forged Nicholson signature by Joseph Cosey

In addition, Cosey used the terminology, "Paid out," which did not come into usage until long after the purported date of the document, 1786. And the content of the document also betrays its falseness; it orders payment to Silas Hill, "being due him for services and attendance as a member of Congress." No one by this name has ever served in Congress.

105 A genuine signature of David Rittenhouse

106 A forged Rittenhouse signature

ABRAHAM LINCOLN

In the genuine autograph letter of Abraham Lincoln, the handwriting shows a strong and bold writing style with frequent forceful pressure on the pen causing wide, bold pen strokes. The letter also reveals evidence of having been written with a fluid, quick movement of the hand as Lincoln rapidly moved from letter to letter and from word to word [107].

I would suggest that
Hon. Stephen T. Logan, of Springfield, Illinois, and Col. James
Mitchell, of Freehole, in the
same State, be appointed as
Commission to examine
into claims. &c. at Cairo—
the said Commissioners to
have the same power
as the late Commissioners
at Lewis.
I would also suggest
that John R. Shepley. Esq of St.
Lewis be selected as attorney
to the said Commission.

April. 2. 1862.   A Lincoln

107 A genuine autograph letter of Abraham Lincoln
dated April 2, 1862

Crown Point, Ha
Sep. 2, 1862

Gen. Meade —
Please allow this
woman to pass safely over
the lines into Culpepper County,
and return the following day —
For which this shall be her
warrant.
A. Lincoln

Hon. Sec of War
E. M. Stanton, Esq.

Please have this message
dispatched to Gen. Meade, and
give duplicate to the bearer,
Mrs. Morehead, a widow of
Culpepper County
Sep. 2, 1862   A. Lincoln

108 A forged Lincoln letter by Joseph Cosey

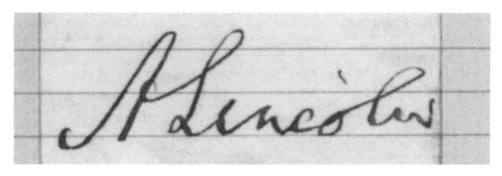

109 An enlargement of a genuine signature of Abraham Lincoln

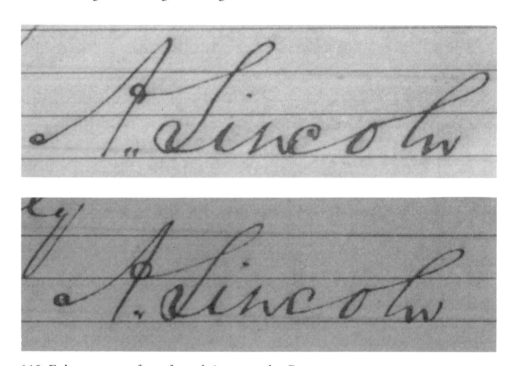

110 Enlargements of two forged signatures by Cosey

While Joseph Cosey is perhaps the most skillful forger of Abraham Lincoln, his forgeries are apparent even before comparing individual letters or words. His forged letter [108] is written with much care, without the quick motion seen in Lincoln's letter [107]. The pen pressure is much lighter and hesitant, particularly in the signature. The clear pattern seen in Lincoln's handwriting of the letters and words moving to the right is not seen in the forgery; instead the movement is more vertical, each word being individually written with no sense of movement toward the next word.

A curious habit of Lincoln's was to always write his signature with the *ln* higher than the *nco*. This is clearly seen here [109]; equally clear is Cosey's failure to note this characteristic [110].

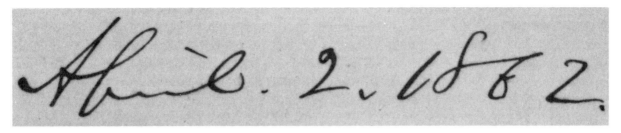

111 The date *April 2, 1862* written by Abraham Lincoln

112 The date *September 2, 1862* written by Cosey

Differences in the writing of numbers are also revealed in the dates; the *2* in the dates is written quite differently, while the *6* is slanted by Lincoln and the *1* has a tail when written by Lincoln [111, 112].

Other differences are shown in the following letters and words: the capitals *C*, *F*, and *S* [113]; lower case *th* and *w*; and the words *and*, *the*, *to*, and *of* [114].

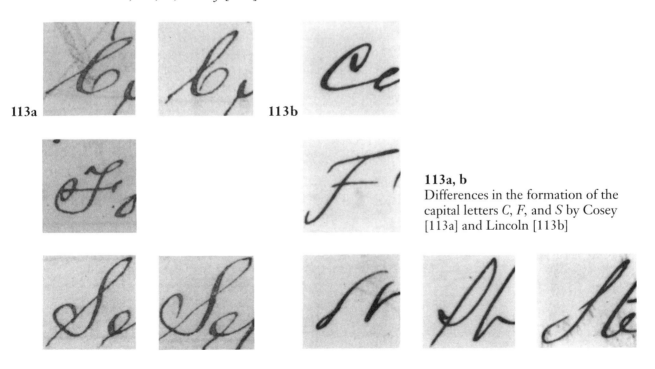

113a

113b

113a, b
Differences in the formation of the capital letters *C*, *F*, and *S* by Cosey [113a] and Lincoln [113b]

114a, b Differences in the formation of the letters *th* and *w;* and the words *and, the, to,* and *of* by Cosey [114a] and Lincoln [114b]

Having completed his work, Cosey was evidently not concentrating when he wrote the final date, making the *2* much too small. His overwriting is quite obvious and would be highly unusual in genuine writing [115]. Finally, the shakiness of Cosey's handwriting is seen in several examples from the forgery [116].

The historical information in a questioned piece can also be a decisive factor in uncovering a fraud. For example, on the date of this forgery, September 2, 1862, Lincoln was in Washington, and it is highly unlikely he would have gone to Crown Point, Virginia, the same day.

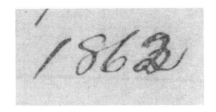

115 Cosey has written over the number *2* in the date *1862*

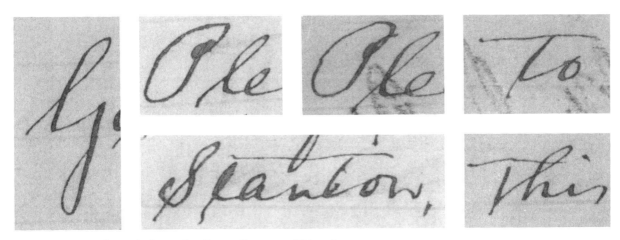

116 Letters and words from the Cosey forgery of Lincoln, showing shakiness in the writing

GEORGE WASHINGTON

Washington's writing has a sharpness and crispness with a very consistent flow, particularly in the upper loops of the *h* and *l*, and his letter formations are very distinctive. These characteristics are revealed in the examples of his genuine signatures and his handwriting [117, 118].

117 Genuine signatures of George Washington

The General presents his best respects to Doctr. Morgan — upon enquiry of Colonel Mifflin, concerning the Horse (the Doctr. very kindly made a tender of to him) he is given to understand, that this Horse did not belong to the King, or any of his Officers; but was the property of a Doctr. Loyd, an avow'd Enemy to the American Cause — As the General does not know under what ~~bound of~~ predicament the property of these kind of People may fall; In short, if there was no kind of doubt in the case, as the Horse is of too much value for the General to think of robbing the Doctr. of, he begs leave to return him; accompanied with sincere thanks for the politeness with which he was presented; and his request, that the Doctr. will not think the General meant to slight his favours. —

He is sorry to hear of Mrs. Morgan's Indisposition — hopes she is better to day. —

Friday — Morning.
22d. Mar. 1776.

118 A genuine letter of George Washington, dated March 22,
1776, completely in his hand, written in the third person

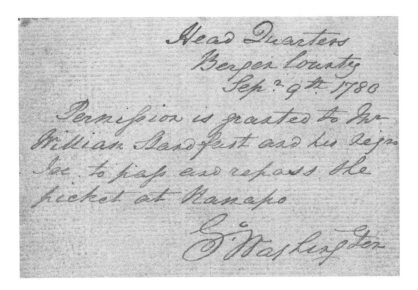

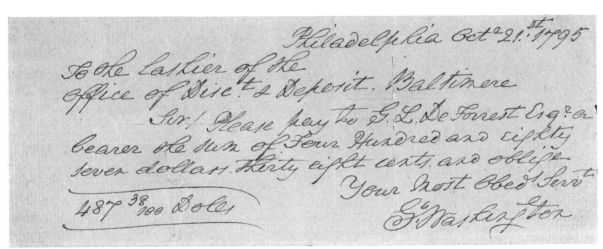

119, 120
Two forgeries of George
Washington by Robert Spring

Robert Spring's forgeries of George Washington are excellently accomplished, but he has not replicated the sharpness of the angles in Washington's writing, and he has exaggerated several of the characteristics of Washington's handwriting, notably the size of the upper loop of the *h* when following a *t* [119, 120]. The following illustrations further show the differences between the two hands [121-130].

121a, b
The capital *W* in Washington's signature. The peaks are pointed in the genuine signatures [121a] and rounded in the forgeries [121b]

121a

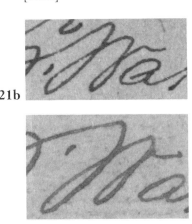

121b

122a

122b

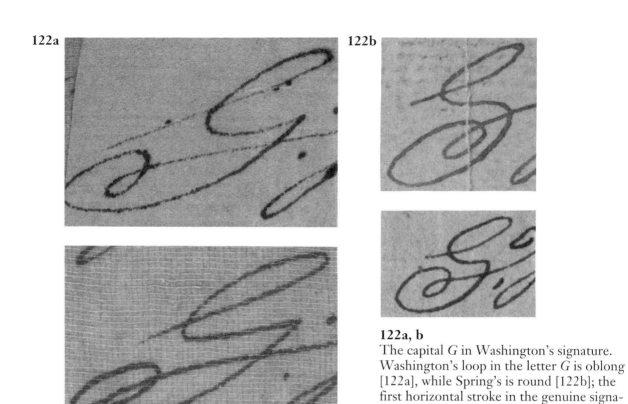

122a, b
The capital *G* in Washington's signature. Washington's loop in the letter *G* is oblong [122a], while Spring's is round [122b]; the first horizontal stroke in the genuine signature changes direction at a sharp point, while the forged *G* has a rounded downward turn.

123a

123b

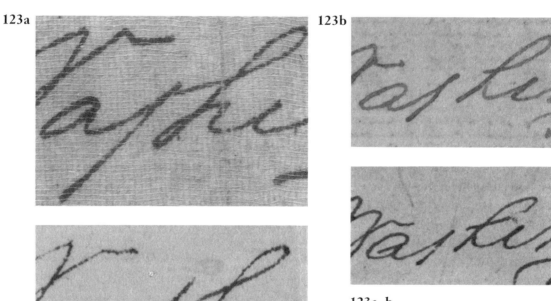

123a, b
The *ash* in Washington's signature. Washington always brings the *s* well below the baseline [123a], a habit Spring did not follow [123b]. Washington either begins the *h* touching the *s* or almost touching it; the forger has left a distinct gap.

124a

124b

124a, b
The lower case *g* in Washington's signature.
Washington crosses the lower part of the *g* with
a curved line at the bottom of the stroke [124a].
Spring makes the cross midway [124b].

125a A genuine capital *C*

125b Forged capital *C*'s

126a Genuine capital *D*'s

126b Forged capital *D*'s

127a Genuine capital *G*'s

127b A forged capital *G*

128a Genuine examples of Washington's capital *H*'s

128b Forged capital *H*'s by Robert Spring

  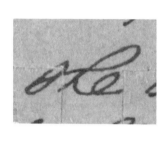 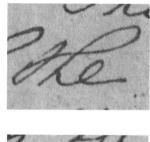

   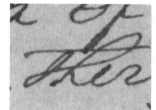

129a Genuine examples of the letters *th*

129b Forged examples of the letters *th*

   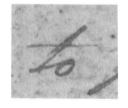

130a Genuine examples of the word *to*

130b A forged example of the word *to*

ROBERT BURNS

Antique Smith was one of the most accomplished forgers, but his work is very uneven in quality. The largest collection of his forgeries is in the National Library of Scotland, and an examination of them makes one wonder why he was so inconsistent. Seeing one of his mediocre examples can leave an examiner overly confident when confronted with one of his better creations.

Alexander Howland Smith began forging letters and manuscripts of Robert Burns and Sir Walter Scott in the 1880s. Working in Edinburgh, Smith created plausible stories of where the pieces came from and was able to sell a large number. He soon added other notable names to his list of creations, but Burns and Scott were his mainstays, so much so that the number he put onto the market in Edinburgh and London raised suspicions.

In mid-1892, these suspicions came to a head with the publication of a Burns letter that many thought contained a text that was too uncharacteristic of Burns. A great debate erupted in the pages of the *Edinburgh Dispatch*, which originally had set out to prove the letter in question genuine. By the end of 1892, the evidence of forgery was overwhelming and Smith was arrested, his "literary" career at an end.

Genuine writing of Robert Burns is unusually clear, with the appearance of having been written with great care. In many respects it has a number of the characteristics of a forgery: letters individually written and not linked to others, unusual pen pressure patterns and a drawn appearance [131]. There are also other characteristics that can be used to differentiate the genuine from the forged.

When the Burns forgery by Antique Smith is compared with the genuine example, the most obvious difference is the "tightness" of the writing. Burns's writing is much more open. There is less space between letters and words, and Smith's writing is slightly smaller — a common habit of many forgers. These as well as differences in letter patterns between Burns's handwriting and Smith's fabricated attempts are revealed in the following illustrations [131-143].

One of the very few errors Smith did make with some consistency was to endorse letters in the same handwriting as the body of the letter when it should have been in the hand of the recipient. However, when Smith was at his best, his skill was extraordinary [132].

Robert Burns

22

I bless & praise thy matchless might,
When thousands thou has left in night,
That I am here before thy sight,
        For gifts & grace,
A burning & a shining light
        To a' this place. —

What was I, or my generation,
That I should get such exaltation?
I, wha deserv'd most just damnation,
        For broken laws
Sax thousand years ere my creation,
        Thro' Adam's cause!
When from my mother's womb I fell,
Thou might hae plunged me deep in hell,
To gnash my gooms, & weep, & wail,
        In burning lakes,
Where damned devils roar & yell
        Chain'd to their stakes. —
Yet I am here, a chosen sample,
To shew thy grace is great & ample:
I'm here, a pillar o' thy temple
        Strong as a rock,
A guide, a ruler & example
        To a' thy flock. —

131 A genuine signature from a letter of Robert Burns
    and a genuine autograph manuscript

O The Brigs of Ayr.———

To John Ballantyne Esquire, this poem is dedicated
by his most obliged and humble Servant
Robt. Burns.

To John Maitland Esq.   SPURIOUS

I append herein the annexed poem as a recom-
-pence for my delay in not writing you sooner than now.—
will remind you of many a pleasant hour in our town
Ayr, and I hope you will accept this copy in the spirit
of gratitude in which it is sent.
Robt. Burns.

O The simple Bard, rough at the rustic plough,
Learning his tuneful trade from every bough;
O The chanting linnet, or the mellow thrush,
Hailing the setting sun, sweet in the green thorn bush;
O The soaring lark, the perching redbreast shrill,
Or deep toned plovers, grey, wild whistling o'er the hill;
Shall he, nurst in the peasants lowly shed,
O To hardy independence bravely bred,
By early Poverty to hardship stee'led
And trained to arms in stern Misfortune's field
Shall he be guilty of their hireling crimes,
The servile, mercenary, swiss of rhymes?
Or labour hard the panegyric close,
With all the venal soul of dedicating prose?

132 A forgery of a Robert Burns letter and manuscript from
the collection of the National Library of Scotland

  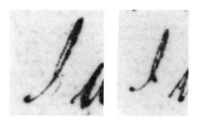

133a Burns's loops in the capital *I* are well defined and rounded.

133b By contrast, Smith forms elongated, almost imperceptible loops.

134a Burns's downstrokes in the capital *T* end in a hook to the left.

134b Smith's downstrokes in the capital *T* end in a curve to the left.

 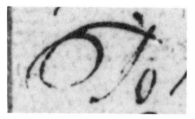     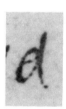

135a Burns's *d*'s have long ascenders.

135b Smith's *d* ascenders are short.

135c
Burns also writes a variant form of the *d* with a curved ascender, which Smith does not use at all.

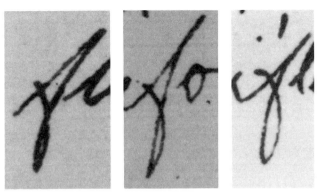 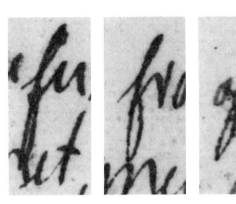

136a The ending of Burns's *f* stroke crosses the downstroke as well as the ascending stroke.

136b The ending of Smith's *f* stroke crosses the downstroke only slightly.

       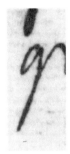

137a The shape of Burns's *g* bowl is consistent, and the descender is looped generously.

137b Smith's *g* bowl varies in shape, and the loop is lean and narrow.

138a Burns's *l* slants to the right.

138b Smith's *l* is written vertically.

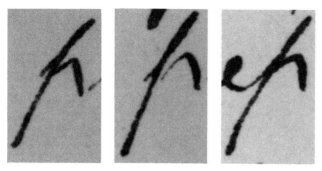

139a Burns's *p* descenders are long.

139b Smith's *p* descenders are short.

140a The start of Burns's *s* stroke begins at the line or above it, and the end of the stroke crosses the ascending stroke.

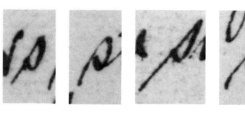

140b The start of Smith's *s* stroke often begins below the line, and the end of the stroke does not cross the ascending stroke.

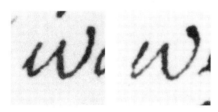

141a Burns's *w* stroke starts above the baseline or at the top.

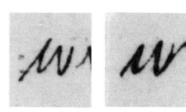

141b Smith's *w* stroke starts below or at the baseline.

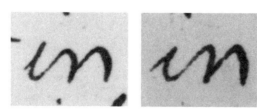

142a Burns writes the word *in* with open, round loops.

142b Smith's word *in* is tightly written, with pointed loops.

143a A genuine signature of Robert Burns

143b
A forged Burns signature
by Antique Smith

143a, b The *B* in the signature written by Smith is much wider
than in Burns's example. In addition, the *u* and *s* in
Burns's signature begins below the baseline, whereas in the
Smith forgery they do not.

6

"Authorized" Forgeries

SECRETARIAL SIGNATURES

Many people in prominent positions, who are required to sign numerous letters and documents, have at one time or another authorized others to sign their names for them. In most instances there was no intention to deceive the recipient by attempting to imitate the signature, the normal practice being for the proxy signer to place his own initials after the secretarial signature. While one does need to be aware of such secretarial or proxy signatures, these are not what we are concerned with in collecting historical letters and documents.

"Authorized" forgeries in which a signature is imitated in an attempt to deceive the recipient into believing it was signed by the person named generally began about the turn of the twentieth century. There were, of course, earlier exceptions, but it was not until about 1900 that it became somewhat commonplace to be deceptive about secretarial signatures.

In eighteenth-century France, kings rarely signed routine official documents as their relatively simple signatures were imitated by *secrétaires de main*. In many instances an arrow was drawn from the royal "signature" to that of the secretary below [144]. This custom cannot, however, always be relied upon because many secretaries omitted the line or arrow. Unless the royal signature is very distinctly genuine, which is unusual, all such signatures are suspect. These secretarially signed documents must have been treated with less authority than intended as the kings and queens, especially Marie Antoinette, took to adding notes and a second, genuine, royal signature [145].

More deceptive are the "Bonaparte" signatures signed on documents by his secretary of state, Hughes Maret, when Bonaparte was First Consul [146-148]. Other than documents of this type, Napoleon did not authorize others to sign for him.

144 A Louis XVI document, with the arrow drawn from the royal "signature" to that of the secretary (opposite page)

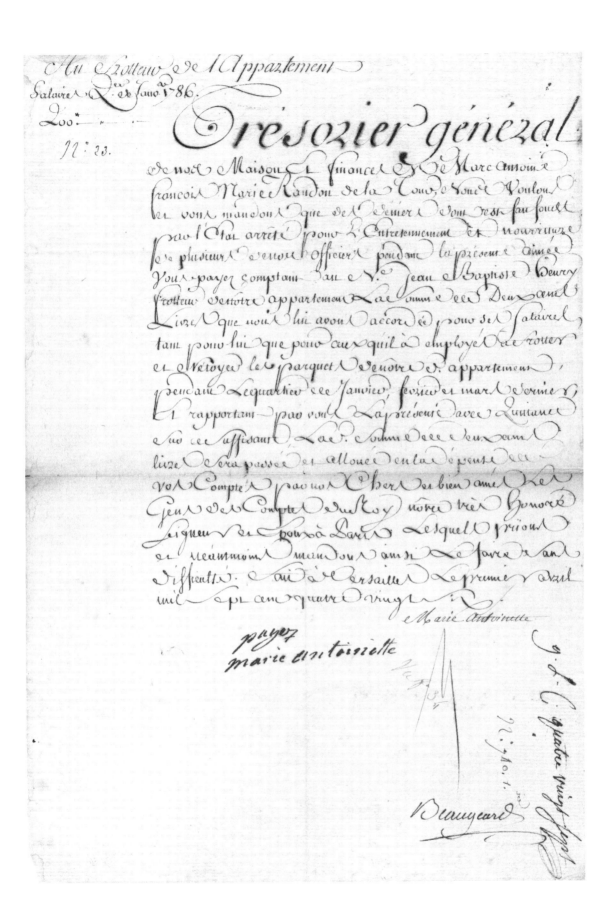

Au Frotteur de l'Appartement

Salaire du 1er Janvier 1786.

200.ᵗ

N° 23.

Trésorier général

de notre Maison et finances Sr. De Marc Antoine
François Marie Randon de la Tour, et donné Voulons
et vous mandons que des deniers de votre reste faisons
par l'État arrêté pour l'entretiennement et nourriture
de plusieurs de notre officiers pendant la présente année
Vous payez comptant au Sr. Jean Baptiste Henry
Frotteur de notre appartement la somme de Deux cent
Livres que nous lui avons accordé pour ses salaires
tant pour lui que pour ceux qu'il a employés à frotter
et nettoyer les parquets de notre dit appartement
pendant le quartier de Janvier, février et mars de nie
et rapportant par vous la présente avec quittance
sur ce suffisant. La dite somme de deux cent
livres sera passée et allouée en la dépense de
vos comptes par nos chers et bien amés les
Gens des comptes du Roy notre très honoré
Seigneur et époux à Paris, lesquels prions
et néanmoins mandons ainsi le faire sans
difficulté. Fait à Versailles le premier avril
mil sept cent quatre vingt.

Marie Antoinette

payez
marie antoinette

Beaugeard

91

De Par Le Roy

Il est ordonné au Commis particulier
du Trésorier général de la Guerre à Lyon
de payer au N:ᵉ Gidr Cavalier de M:ᵉ à la résidence de Lyon
la somme de *Cinquante livres* pour l'indemniser des frais de
la capture de Charles Feüe soldat déserteur de la Division de Toulon
Corps-Royal de Marine. Il retiendra sur cette somme les Quatre deniers
pour livre et Cinq sous pour le contrôle de la Quittance en parcha[min]
qu'il retirera dudit Cavalier. Il adressera ladite Quittance
le présent Ordre au Trésorier général de la Guerre à Paris,
en fera le remplacement, et qui s'entendra pour son remboursement avec
Trésorier général de la Marine.

Fait à Versailles le 16. Mars 1783.

Louis

459

92

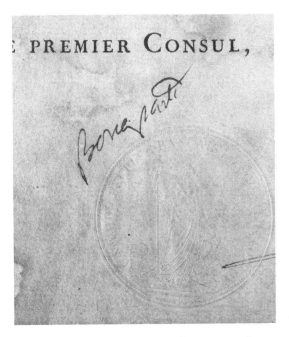

146 A secretarial signature of Bonaparte by his secretary of state, Hughes Maret, when Bonaparte was First Consul

148 Another document of Napoleon Bonaparte with a secretarial signature by Maret (right)

145
A document of Marie Antoinette signed with a second and genuine royal signature (opposite page)

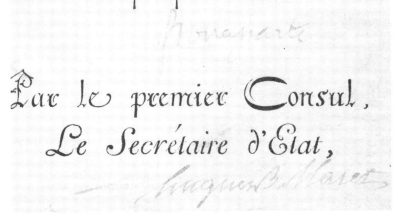

147 A secretarial signature of Bonaparte by Maret, below which is Maret's genuine signature

THE UNITED STATES OF AMERICA.

To all to whom these Presents shall come, Greeting:

WHEREAS *William Alfred Sykes and James Turner Sykes of Morgan County Alabama* ha__ deposited in the GENERAL LAND OFFICE of the United States, a Certificate of the REGISTER OF THE LAND OFFICE at *Huntsville* whereby it appears that full payment has been made by the said *William Alfred Sykes and James Turner Sykes* according to the provisions of the Act of Congress of the 24th of April, 1820, entitled "*An Act making further provision for the sale of the Public Lands*," for *the North west quarter of Section nine in Township five of Range four West in the District of Lands subject to sale at Huntsville Alabama Containing one hundred and Sixty Acres*

—— *according to the official plat of the survey of the said Lands, returned to the General Land Office by the* SURVEYOR GENERAL, *which said tract has been purchased by the said William Alfred Sykes and James Turner Sykes* NOW KNOW YE, *That the* UNITED STATES OF AMERICA, *in consideration of the Premises, and in conformity with the several Acts of Congress, in such case made and provided,* HAVE GIVEN AND GRANTED, *and by these presents* DO GIVE AND GRANT, *unto the said William Alfred Sykes and James Turner Sykes and to their heirs, the said tract above described:* TO HAVE AND TO HOLD *the same, together with all the rights, privileges, immunities, and appurtenances of whatsoever nature, thereunto belonging, unto the said William Alfred Sykes and James Turner Sykes and to their heirs and assigns forever. as tenants in Common and not as joint tenants* IN TESTIMONY WHEREOF, I, *Andrew Jackson* PRESIDENT OF THE UNITED STATES OF AMERICA, *have caused these letters to be made* PATENT, *and the* SEAL *of the* GENERAL LAND OFFICE *to be hereunto affixed.*

GIVEN *under my hand, at the* CITY OF WASHINGTON, *the sixteenth day of October in the Year of our Lord one thousand eight hundred and thirty five and of the* INDEPENDENCE OF THE UNITED STATES *the Sixtieth*

BY THE PRESIDENT: *Andrew Jackson*

Edward Brown COMMISSIONER OF THE GENERAL LAND OFFICE.

Recorded, Vol. ___ Page *351 Etc*

149 A presidential land grant signed by Andrew Jackson's secretary. Presidential land grants, beginning with the mid-term of Jackson's administration and continuing with the succeeding presidents, were signed by their respective secretaries.

In America, little or no effort was made to imitate the presidents' signatures when secretaries were authorized to sign presidential land grants partway through Andrew Jackson's administration. Despite the very clear statement on this type of document indicating a secretarial signature, these continue to be the most common type of secretarially signed documents offered for sale as genuine [149].

150
A genuine Texas treasury warrant ordering payment for someone to sign the name of the president of the Republic of Texas, Sam Houston

The president of Texas, Sam Houston, found the signing of exchequer bills too burdensome a task and authorized the hiring of someone to sign them for him [150]. These signatures are not, however, similar enough to the Texan's flamboyant signature to cause confusion.

Some wives, for instance, so commonly wrote and signed their husbands' correspondence that letters penned by them are frequently mistaken for their illustrious husbands' penmanship. The most deceptive was the English poet William Wordsworth's wife, Mary [151], followed many years later by Varina Davis who imitated Jefferson Davis's handwriting so well that only the period she placed after her ver-sions is an immediate sign that she and not her husband wrote them [154].

While several American presidents from the early part of the nineteenth century authorized secretaries to sign routine nonofficial documents for them, it was not until Andrew Johnson's time, in 1865, that really deceptive official documents appear. Johnson, two months after becoming president, began the practice of having military and naval appointments bear a stamped signature that can be very misleading to the uninformed.

151 A signature of William Wordsworth by his wife, Mary

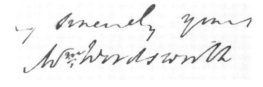

152 A genuine signature of the poet

153 A genuine signature of Jefferson Davis

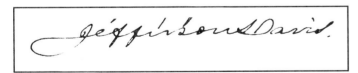

154 Two signatures of the Confederate president by his wife, Varina, who added a period after the signatures as a subtle mark of her authorship

Theodore Roosevelt frequently employed a rubber stamp before becoming president, but even an untrained eye cannot mistake its true nature [156]. The secretary who wrote and signed the letter illustrated here was much more deceptive [157]. The secretary who signed for William Howard Taft, however, could not deceive anyone who has a genuine signature with which to compare it [159], nor should anyone be fooled by Woodrow Wilson's rubber-stamped signature when he was governor of New Jersey, 1911-1913 [161].

155
A genuine signature of
Theodore Roosevelt

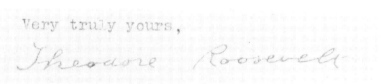

156
A rubber stamp signature
of Roosevelt

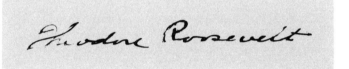

157
A secretarial signature
of Roosevelt

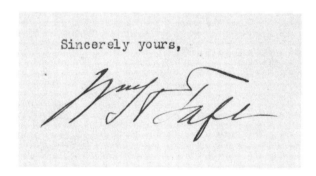

158 A genuine signature of William Howard Taft

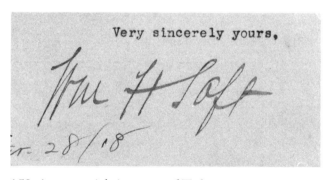

159 A secretarial signature of Taft

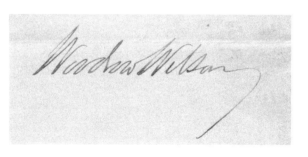

160 A genuine signature of Woodrow Wilson

161 A rubber stamp signature of Wilson

George B. Christian, Warren G. Harding's secretary, was a different matter. He signed so many of Harding's letters that for many years it was not understood which were the genuinely signed examples [163]. This practice was discontinued when Harding entered the White House. Calvin Coolidge's secretary, when Coolidge was governor of Massachusetts, made a serious attempt at imitating the characteristics of his writing. Like his predecessors, though, Coolidge personally signed all White House letters [165].

Later in the decade, Herbert Hoover, as Secretary of Commerce, employed one A. G. Shankey who became very proficient at imitating her boss's signature, so much so that she boasted of it in a letter to Christian Herter [167, 168].

162 A genuine signature of Warren G. Harding

163 A secretarial signature of Harding by George B. Christian

164
A genuine signature of Calvin Coolidge

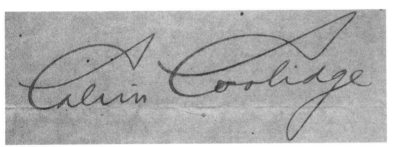

165
A signature of Coolidge by his secretary when he was governor of Massachusetts

166 A genuine signature of Herbert Hoover

167 A signature of Hoover by his secretary, A. G. Shankey

168 A postscript on a letter by Shankey noting her skill at signing Hoover's name

97

Franklin D. Roosevelt, before becoming president, employed a number of persons to sign his name, commencing with his first position, Assistant Secretary of the Navy. The illustrations below show the work of some of these secretaries [169]. Three genuine signatures appear on the following page [170].

169 Signatures of Franklin D. Roosevelt by various secretaries

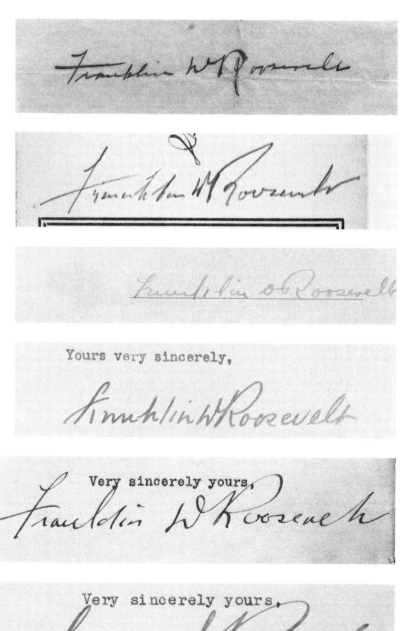

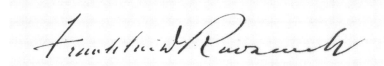

Except for a few brief periods Harry Truman always wrote his own signature [171], and when, as president, he did authorize a secretarial version on White House cards, a period was added after the *S* [172].

171
A genuine signature of
Harry S Truman

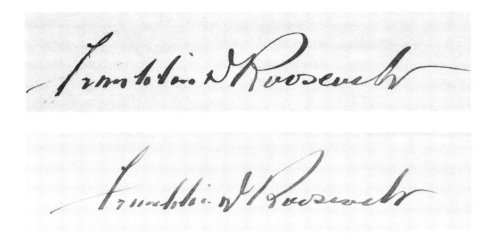

172
A secretarial signature
of President Truman
on a White House card

Dwight D. Eisenhower was the last president who did not allow secretaries and machines to sign his name extensively. Even during the Second World War, Eisenhower signed all of the letters that were written in his name. In a letter to his wife, he wrote that it was simply impossible for him to keep up with the volume of correspondence and that while his letters had to be composed by secretaries, he personally signed every one. It was necessary for Eisenhower, while he was president of Columbia University and during the first presidential campaign, in the fall of 1952, to authorize a secretary to sign his name, as well as use a machine to write his signature. It was not until the last years of his life that he again authorized a secretary to sign his name but this time with the middle initial omitted [174].

173 Genuine signatures of Dwight D. Eisenhower

174 Secretarial signatures of Eisenhower

John F. Kennedy may have been credited with bringing a new atmosphere to Washington, but he also brought the practice of rarely signing one's name personally. Beginning with his first years in Washington and continuing through his presidency, he authorized more than a dozen secretaries to sign his name and also extensively used signing machines with many different writing patterns [176]. This same policy has been carried on, in varying degrees, by all of Kennedy's successors.

175 Genuine signatures of
    John F. Kennedy

176 Secretarial signatures of Kennedy

177 A genuine draft of a letter written by Ronald Reagan when he was governor of California, instructing his secretary to "sign it Dutch" after she had typed it on official stationery

The practice is now so common and well established that even though Ronald Reagan frequently drafted letters in his own handwriting, these drafts were then typed and a machine signature added. In 1986, a group of these drafts was uncovered. The drafts showed Reagan's habit when he was governor of California of taking the time personally to write long, detailed and very articulate responses to letters. His secretary would then type them on official stationery and apply the signature appropriate to the manner in which he signed the draft. The letter reproduced here represents the ultimate in his attitude toward having machine signatures: a letter reassuring old friends of his continued accessibility with a note for his secretary to "sign it Dutch" [177]. Reagan's missives are no more likely to be genuine when written from his movie star days. The friendly two-page letter below, written in 1949, despite its very personal nature, was actually written and signed by his mother, employed at that time by Warner Brothers to answer all of his correspondence [178].

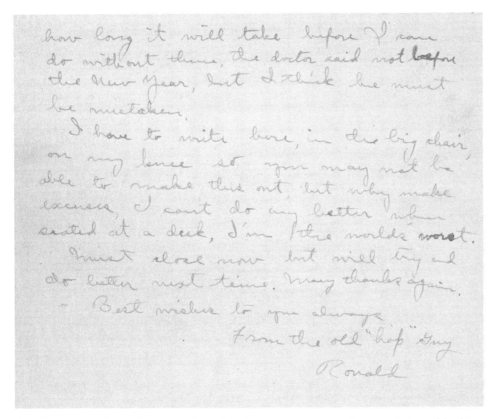

178 A letter of Ronald Reagan from his days as an actor, written and signed by his mother, who was employed by Warner Brothers to handle his correspondence

Public officials are not the only ones who authorized deceptive signatures. The following illustrations represent a very small sampling of genuine signatures, along with the signatures of those who have been given the secretarial task without indicating this to the recipient [179].

179a-e
Examples of genuine and secretarial signatures of various noted personalities (continued verso)

Genuine signatures

Secretarial signatures

179a George M. Cohan

179b Clarence Darrow

Genuine signatures

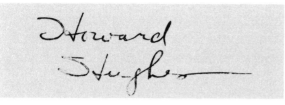

Secretarial signatures

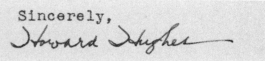

179c Howard Hughes

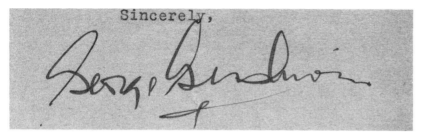

179d George Gershwin

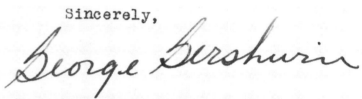

179e Walt Disney

AUTOPEN SIGNATURES

Many have assumed that the world of historical letters and documents would be affected by the word processor, but the word processor is not the first invention of the computer age to have a serious impact on collecting.

The deceptive use of machines that, based upon a matrix of a genuine signature, sign a person's name with a pen, which duplicates the unevenness of genuine writing, has revolutionized the collecting of modern presidential letters. Unless there is strong evidence to the contrary, it should be assumed that any letter from a president since 1960 does not bear a genuine signature (although the letter may be genuine). President Kennedy and his successors had many different signature patterns in use, and a collector could have half a dozen letters all bearing different signatures which could still have been signed by machines. Presidents Ford and Carter, prior to their presidency, had refused the use of such machines, but the pressure of the tremendous volume of mail was sufficient to change their minds.

It should always be assumed that any letter, signed photograph, or other piece not of a truly personal or important business nature could have been signed by a machine if it is from a well-known person who receives many routine letters requiring an answer. The astronauts, for example, found it necessary to resort to machine signatures on the souvenirs sent out from NASA headquarters.

The original autopen machine has been supplanted in recent years by a more sophisticated machine. The only certain way of determining whether a piece is signed by machine is to obtain another identical signature or handwriting pattern and to place one on top of the other to confirm their common machine origin.

A number of books and monographs have reproduced the known machine signature patterns of modern presidents and must be consulted when examining presidential material after 1960 (see the bibliography).

7

The Hitler Diaries: Bad Forgeries but a Great Hoax

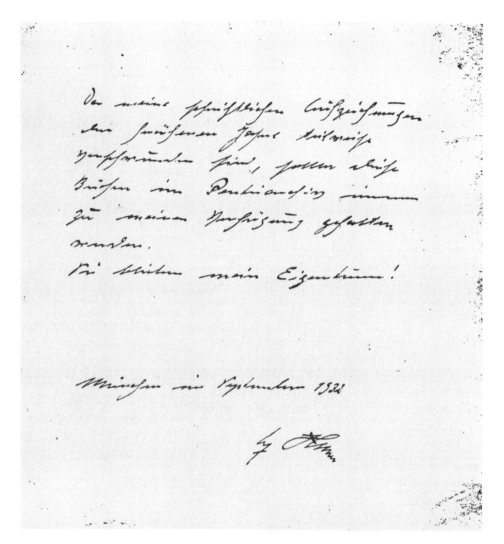

180 A page dated September 1932 from the forged Hitler diaries

On Sunday night, May 1, 1983, I was reading a proof copy of the next day's *Newsweek* in the bar of the Ritz Carlton Hotel in Washington, D.C. I was awaiting the arrival of *Newsweek*'s editor, Maynard Parker, with whom I would be appearing that evening on a national news discussion program. Having steadfastly avoided publicity in the past and after initially refusing *Newsweek*'s overtures, I had finally agreed to work with them as their special consultant on the Hitler diaries. As I reflected on the previous week's news stories, the bizarreness of the circus created by the historians and journalists stunned me. The thrust of the news media's coverage should have been on the need to examine the diaries physically. Unfortunately, it was diffused into speculations, many wild and absurd, of historians and others. After seeing the illustrations in *Stern*'s first issue several days before, it was evident that the diaries illustrated, and probably all of the others, were fake; I needed only to examine the physical evidence of all the diaries to prove this conclusively and complete my assignment for *Newsweek*. Being unfamiliar with the needs and criteria of the news media, I could not understand the public attention being given to the Hitler diaries story. More important, I could not understand how a major European publishing house had been swindled out of more than $5 million. How could *Newsweek*, the Rupert Murdoch organization, *Paris Match*, and others have invested so much time, effort, and money pursuing publication rights to such outrageous fakes? How had such bad forgeries become such a great hoax?

The paper, ink, and handwriting were not the key elements in the success of the Hitler diaries hoax. The human elements of ambition, secrecy, and greed propelled these inept forgeries into a major journalistic scandal. For the hoax to be successful it was necessary to overcome many journalistic business checkpoints, and this had been accomplished through the emotional reactions of the victims themselves. At many points the hoax could have and should have unraveled, but once out of the hands of the forger, the victims carried the hoax onto the front pages of magazines and newspapers throughout the world.

Konrad Kujau, a Stuttgart dealer in military memorabilia and documents, has pleaded guilty to forging the Hitler diaries [183]. The ineptness and audacity of Kujau has been overshadowed by the gullibility, naïveté, greed, and just plain stupidity of *Stern*'s reporter, Gerd Heidemann. Both were sentenced to four-and-a-half-year prison terms for their roles in the fraud. Their trials were as much an indictment of *Stern*'s management.

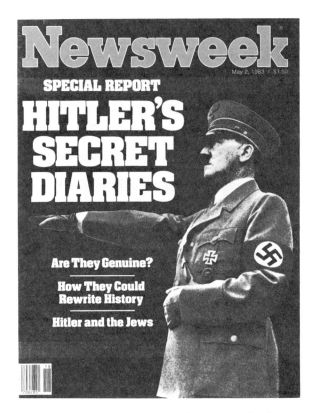

181 The May 2, 1983, issue of *Newsweek* broke the story of Hitler's secret diaries.

The story of the Hitler diaries begins in 1973 when Heidemann, *Stern*'s investigative reporter, known as *Der Spurhund* (The Bloodhound), bought Hermann Goering's yacht, the *Carin II*.

His purchase of this yacht, in need of extensive repairs, is in keeping with his lack of common sense in his journalistic pursuits. At *Stern* he was considered a very thorough researcher — too thorough. He had no sense of when to stop. Editors would find that he had spent many months futilely pursuing a point of no great importance in an investigation. He was also considered extremely gullible, never questioning information given to him. It is a wonder he was not fired years before, but as we will see later, he seems to have been very adept in dealing with *Stern*'s bureaucracy.

The *Carin II* was a financial nightmare for Heidemann. He had mortgaged his house to pay for it and had no funds to restore it. Its ownership did, however, lead him into the world of retired Nazis, including an alleged affair with Goering's daughter, Edda. The boat became the meeting site for many characters from the Third Reich, including former SS Generals Wilhelm Mohnke and Karl Wolff, and the intensity of the reminiscing convinced Heidemann and *Stern* that these "deck conversations" would be a viable book. For some time, he taped the conversations, but they lacked sufficient substance and the book project was abandoned. Heidemann had, however, received a large advance for the book, all of which was spent on the boat.

In 1979, Heidemann married a woman who apparently shared his interest in the Third Reich, and the newlyweds had what they undoubtedly considered a romantic and charming honeymoon in South America at *Stern*'s expense. They were accompanied by SS General Wolff, and the threesome pursued both Mengele and Bormann while visiting with the likes of Walter Rauf and Klaus Barbie.

Upon his return Heidemann faced strong criticism within *Stern* for pursuing Bormann; *Stern* itself had published a major story giving conclusive proof that Hitler's former secretary was killed during the Russian assault on Berlin. He was also forced to face the financial reality that he could no longer keep up Goering's former yacht.

Efforts to sell the boat led him to a major collector of Nazi memorabilia, Fritz Steifel. Steifel decided not to pursue the purchase of the yacht, but in the course of Heidemann's visit the reporter was shown one of Steifel's prized possessions — a diary written by Hitler. It came, he stated, from a plane crash during the final days of the war.

The provenance of the diary was apparently a reasonable deduction by Steifel. He did not realize it was something created by his source, the forger Konrad Kujau. It was to be the first of many pieces of the puzzle that was fitted into place by the victims while the forger, unable to answer their inquiries, simply confirmed the answers they themselves came up with. The provenance was logical because it was well documented that Hitler sent ten metal trunks of papers out of Berlin for Berchtesgaden just as Berlin was falling to the Russians. Hans Baur, Hitler's personal pilot, in his memoirs published years before in the 1950s, describes Hitler's reaction when he told him that a particular airplane had been lost during the final days. Hitler was extremely upset and agitated, yelling that all of the papers created for his posterity had been on that plane. The site of the crash and the fate of these papers were unknown, despite extensive research by at least one writer in the early 1970s. (The airplane almost certainly contained the transcripts of Hitler's meeting with his generals — transcripts that Hitler had ordered to be made to document the incompetency of his military advisers.)

Gerd Heidemann reported seeing the Hitler diary to his editors and was told by Henri Nannen, the founder and publisher of *Stern*, that he did not "want to hear or read about your Nazi crap." Editor Peter Koch was even more blunt: his memo forbade Heidemann to pursue any Nazi stories and called Heidemann "mentally deranged." Rational people would assume this would be the end of Heidemann's enterprise, but Heidemann was able to "disappear" in a sense, with the editors not caring what he was doing as long as they did not have to deal with him or publish his stories. Heidemann, being such a problem, was not assigned to any department, and it seems no one wanted to raise the issue of what he was doing out of fear he would be assigned to them. Thomas Walde, the head of the history section at *Stern*, however, listened to Heidemann's story of the Hitler diary and secretly authorized him, despite the direct and clear orders from the publisher and editor-in-chief, to pursue additional diaries.

After extensive work, Heidemann found the crash site of the airplane, near Börnersdorf in East Germany, and also located the source of Steifel's diary — Konrad Kujau. Kujau had had a very profitable relationship with Steifel and had sold him about $75,000 in Hitler memorabilia, mostly his watercolors and paintings. Steifel had not blindly trusted Kujau; he had hired a reputed art historian named August Priesack who had been employed by the Third Reich to catalog Hitler's watercolors and paintings during 1934-1939. Kujau must have held

182 *Stern*, April 28, 1983, responding to the discovery of Hitler's diaries

his breath while Priesack examined his fakes, and his relief must have been incredible when Priesack not only authenticated them but recalled fondly that he had last seen many of them in the late 1930s!

After listening to Steifel's glowing praise of Kujau, Heidemann had no hesitation in offering Kujau two million deutsche marks for the diaries. Kujau again stated that they had been recovered from the plane crash, the story he had gotten from Steifel, and then created an elaborate story of how his brother, a general in the East German army, knew where the diaries were and would have to smuggle them out of East Germany. Absolute secrecy would have to be maintained, for not only was his brother violating East German law by smuggling the diaries out but the mere possession of Third Reich memorabilia in West Germany was a crime.

Heidemann and Walde now faced the dilemma of how to raise the two million deutsche marks that Kujau had agreed to (the price would escalate as "additional" volumes were found). They could not go to the editors as they had both defied their direct orders and had devoted six months to the project. They decided to go to the supremely self-confident managing director of Gruner und Jahr, *Stern*'s parent company, Manfred Fischer. Fischer did not like Peter Koch and was delighted to scoop his editor by personally securing the Hitler diaries.

At this same time, a second event was taking place which certainly should have exposed the fraud — even if the possibly senile Priesack could not identify genuine Hitler watercolors and paintings. In 1978, Steifel had shown the German historian Eberhard Jäckel, of Stuttgart University, a number of his Hitler manuscripts as well as his diary. Jäckel recalls seeing the diary but was not particularly interested in it. He did, however, print approximately seventy-five of Steifel's forgeries in a book about Hitler's early writings. After publication, it became clear that many, if not all, of these were fakes, and Jäckel published a public apology and explanation, without mentioning Steifel by name. Walde, when he saw this, became alarmed and asked Heidemann to investigate. Instead of calling Jäckel, Heidemann called Kujau who assured him that they could not have come from him.

Fischer authorized the disbursement of large sums in cash, and the diaries began to arrive at *Stern*. Heidemann then negotiated an extraordinary contract with the magazine for the publication of the diaries. He was granted a very large advance, a veto over the historians who would work on the diaries, and a relatively large percentage of the profits from their publication. According to Fischer, Heidemann was also the person in charge of checking the diaries' authenticity — putting him in the role of having a great financial stake in the diaries being genuine. Fischer did not ask Heidemann to account for the monies spent on the diaries. He was simply told how much was needed, and it was immediately given out in cash.

At the same time that Kujau was defrauding Heidemann by selling him fake diaries, Heidemann was cheating Kujau by only giving him a small part of the money *Stern* thought it was paying for the diaries and *Stern*'s management, in turn, was deceiving the editors.

The third opportunity to prove the diaries false occurred when Heidemann, unable to keep the secrecy of the their existence, showed one to SS General Mohnke. This particular diary referred to events that Mohnke was part of, and Mohnke told Heidemann that it could not possibly be genuine because the events did not happen. Heidemann explained to Mohnke that the diary entries must have reflected what Hitler intended to do but never carried out.

In May 1981, Peter Koch wanted to assign Heidemann to investigate the attempted assassination of the pope. He seems to have had no interest in what Heidemann had been doing for the previous several years, but when he ordered Heidemann to go to Turkey, he had to be brought in on the scoop that the managing director of Gruner und Jahr had for the magazine. Koch and the other editors who were let in on the secret were angry but did not question the authenticity of the diaries. Koch stated that he believed they must have been genuine. After all, Fischer had paid millions of dollars for them and it was unthinkable that they had not been authenticated and their provenance proven. Both Nannen and Koch visited Heidemann at home to discuss the diaries, and both were shocked at his incredible lifestyle: he had purchased two new apartments in which to put Hitler memorabilia, he had a new BMW and Porsche, and he told them that he was negotiating to purchase Hitler's boyhood home. Koch was shown, among other pieces of memorabilia, what Heidemann claimed to be Hitler's suicide gun. The problem was that it was both the wrong make and the wrong caliber, but this did not seem to disillusion Koch. Heidemann's source for the pistol was, of course, Konrad Kujau. Despite these visits and the questions they must have raised concerning Heidemann's wealth the hoax continued.

In July 1981, Manfred Fischer moved up to the position of managing director of Bertelsmann, the parent company of Gruner und Jahr, and he was replaced by Gerd Schulte-

183 *Stern*, in its May 19, 1983, issue, reported on Konrad Kujau, the forger of the Hitler diaries.

111

Hillen. Schulte-Hillen, a great admirer of Fischer, never questioned the diaries' authenticity. Fischer, he stated, certainly would never have spent millions of dollars for them unless they had been proven genuine. Schulte-Hillen's main contribution to the continuation of the hoax was his direct order to Peter Koch to treat Heidemann with more respect and to stop speaking so derisively about him and the diaries. Heidemann was given a bonus, and he decided to raise the price he claimed he was paying for the diaries.

By the end of the year, despite an almost complete lack of interest on the part of the editors, Shulte-Hillen decided that it was time to begin publishing the diaries, whether or not all of them had been smuggled out of East Germany. While he thought there certainly could be no question of their authenticity, it was agreed that they would have to bring in outside experts because their genuineness would certainly be questioned by other publications. This, of course, should have been the end of the story, but for various reasons the three experts recommended to *Stern* by the Bundesarchiv (German Federal Archives) all presented reports that either authenticated the pages examined or allowed Stern to interpret them as authenticating the diaries.

The handwriting in the Hitler diaries is certainly the most inept attempt at imitating another's handwriting since William Henry Ireland's absurdly fake Shakespeare manuscripts in the late eighteenth century. With the exception of imitating Hitler's habit of slanting his writing diagonally as he wrote across the page, the forger failed to observe or to imitate the most fundamental characteristics of his handwriting. Obtaining the materials to create the forgeries was accomplished with an equal lack of skill. Even superficial research into Hitler's personal habits would reveal that he always used beautifully bound leather writing folders and desk appointments. The imitation leather notebooks with their crude wax seals are almost comical. The use of a mechanical pencil for many consecutive entries and the consistent use of the same blue-black ink are only overshadowed by such colossal errors as mistaking an *F* for an *A* in selecting the large metal initials to put onto the cover of one diary. (The fact that the initials are in a typeface, Engraver's Old English, declared by the Nazis in the early 1940s as being "too Jewish" was at least an understandable error.)

While inept at creating the diaries themselves, Kujau was very clever in assembling what historians would likely have found if, indeed, trunks of Hitler's personal possessions had survived the war. Among the items supposedly contained in this archive were a number of artworks by Hitler including completed as well as unfinished watercolors, an oil painting dated 1934, drawings of Eva Braun and of his parents, his Iron Cross from the First World War, two other medals received by him for wounds, letters to him from Bormann, Hess, and others, two drafts of letters written by him to unidentified young women, and his outline of the program of the National Socialist German Workers Party.

The three experts engaged by *Stern* magazine to authenticate the Hitler diaries and archive were a Swiss, Dr. Max Frei-Sulzer, Herr Hubner from the Bundesarchiv, and an American, Ordway Hilton, noted for exposing the Clifford Irving/Howard Hughes forgeries. To prevent the disclosure of the diaries' existence, these experts were shown three original pages, not from the actual diaries but from separate journals. Two of these pages contained the text of Hitler's statement concerning Rudolph Hess's flight to England, and the third consisted of the text of a telegram. The pages were selected because their content was historically known to exist and therefore would not arouse suspicion. The handwriting in these pages and the journals themselves were identical in every way with the diaries. None of the experts were told that their opinion of the three pages would be used to prove the authenticity of approximately sixty volumes.

Stern provided all three experts with copies or originals of Hitler's writing that they stated were known to be genuine. Some of the examples were from the German Federal Archives in Koblenz, while the others were obtained from what came to be later referred to as the "*Stern*/Heidemann dossier." The examples from the Bundesarchiv were almost without value for comparison purposes: several were notes in pencil, and the others were only signatures. The examples that the experts relied upon for comparison were those later traced to the *Stern*/Heidemann dossier. These were lengthy handwritten letters and inscribed photographs, all written in the identical hand of the questioned journal pages: that of the forger.

The situation is remarkable for its absurdity. *Stern*, in attempting to accomplish an objective verification of the diaries' authenticity, showed their experts only three pages and gave them for comparison examples provided by their own reporter who had a major stake in the diaries' authenticity. (According to the report of the Board of Inquiry in Hamburg, no one could recall how this mix of genuine and forged examples was selected to be shown to the experts for comparison purposes. I had been told that the three experts had made comparisons based on pieces in the Bundesarchiv alone.)

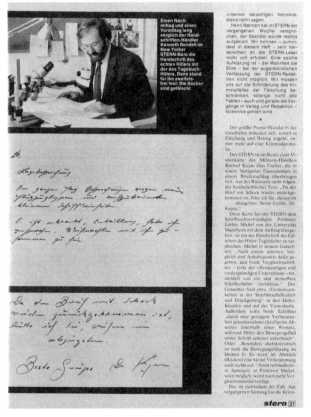

184 Kenneth Rendell at the offices of *Stern* magazine, examining the fake diaries; and two examples of Konrad Kujau's forged writing from the diaries (*Stern*, May 19, 1983)

The three experts, for their part, naïvely accepted *Stern*'s word that what they were being given as genuine examples were indeed that. In two cases the experts noted that there were differences in the signatures of the supposedly genuine examples but stated that the preponderance of evidence provided by the long handwritten letters was sufficient to declare the questioned pages genuine. There seemed to be a complete lack of suspicion on the part of the handwriting experts — an attitude that should always be present in such work.

The importance and relevance of the experts' authentications were significantly enhanced and embellished by *Stern*. In offering the publication rights of the Hitler diaries to various publishing houses, *Stern* dealt with the subject of authentication with the following statement:

> The sensational discovery of the books almost four decades after the collapse of the Third Reich must also create doubt — not only about the credibility of the content, but about the authenticity of the texts in general. *Stern* showed three independent experts an excerpt from the diaries. The origin of the text was not mentioned. The only thing to be examined was whether it had been written by Adolf Hitler personally. As materials for comparison, five samples of Hitler's writing, the authenticity of which is undisputed, were available from the inventories of the Federal Archive in Koblenz. The experts examined not only the writing, but also the content of the text. The famous, officially recognized American expert, Ordway Hilton, by comparing the handwriting between the diary and the Koblenz documents, concluded: "[It] . . . was written by Hitler." Even the experts of the Office of the District Attorney for the state of Rheinland-Pfalz and staff experts for the Federal Archives in Koblenz ascertained on the basis of the documents presented: "With a probability bordering on certainty, the manuscripts in question come from Hitler." And Dr. Max Frei-Sulzer, . . . one of the most prominent European handwriting authorities [stated] . . . "The range of forms and the physiological characteristics of authentic handwriting features and signatures of Adolf Hitler also occur in precisely the same configuration in the documents examined. There can be no doubt that these documents were written by Adolf Hitler personally." The English historian Trevor-Roper , author of *The Last Days of Hitler*, looked the diaries over. [He] considers Heidemann's discovery to be the "most important event of contemporary history within the last decades" and "a journalistic coup without parallel."

This was the statement given to *Newsweek* and other bidders for publication rights. It represented what *Stern*'s editors would like the authentication reports to have said but not what they did say when read in their totality. First of all, the three pages that were "authenticated" were not from the diaries themselves but from separate journals. Whether or not these pages were authentic was only of circumstantial evidence in considering the diaries' authenticity. Most important, the experts were not only given a substantial number of "genuine" items for comparison which did not come from the German Federal Archives, the Bundesarchiv, but which originated either with Heidemann or *Stern* itself. Also directly contradicted in the experts' reports to *Stern* magazine is their statement that conclusions of authenticity were based upon comparison with the Bundesarchiv documents alone. Both Hilton and Frei-Sulzer clearly stated that they principally relied on several lengthy handwriting examples that they identified and that were traced not to the Bundesarchiv group but to the Heidemann/*Stern* dossier. Frei-Sulzer at the end of his report wrote, "in the Heidemann/*Stern* collection we have access to an extremely rich comparative source."

The "authentication" of the diaries by the historians involved was even more inept. They clearly focused on the sensationalism of the story, and not a single historian took the time to investigate properly the content of the diaries. In this area, Kujau was at least more clever than he was at creating the handwriting. He relied on a book, privately printed in 1962-63 by Max Domarus, entitled *Hitler: Speeches and Proclamations, 1932-1945*, and on the Nazi party daily newspaper, the *Volkischer Beobachter*, for his information. It would not have required an exceptionally thorough historian to realize that the daily entries in the diaries coincide exactly with the Domarus work: there are no entries for the days that Domarus did not include.

There are no facts in the diaries that do not appear in these two sources. It is just not conceivable that Hitler's personal diaries would not contain information not found in these two sources. Hitler's own diaries should have included information not found in other works. The subjective comments attributed to Hitler were later criticized by knowledgeable aides and others, but these were, for some time, accepted by both the historians and journalists as being the genuine opinions of their Führer.

These subjective opinions were certainly a conscious effort by Kujau to make the diaries acceptable and salable. While they do present Hitler in a somewhat more favorable light

185 *Newsweek*, May 16, 1983

than many would agree with, he is presented in a way that many Germans born during or after the war can find more palpable. Hitler is portrayed neither as a monster nor as a munificent leader, but rather he is shown as a leader whom the German people put into power at a time of very great economic hardship, a leader who would repudiate the terms imposed upon Germany at the end of the First World War, a leader who might only be guilty of not controlling his fanatical followers. The diaries create a Hitler that many people wanted to believe was real.

The diary entries about the *Kristallnacht*, the nationwide anti-Jewish riots in 1938, are indicative of a new Hitler when he is quoted as complaining about the "fanatics" who have caused "millions and millions in damage to the German economy, and I don't just mean the broken glass." He frequently writes entries concerning the "Jewish problem" but suggests that Germany could ship them to other countries if these countries would accept them. The "final solution" in the diaries was his statement that perhaps Hungary or another area in the East could be given to the Jews so that they could settle there. Heinrich Himmler, the head of the SS, comes under severe criticism by this new Hitler. To quote from *Stern*'s lengthy memo describing the diaries, "Hitler's attitude toward Heinrich Himmler . . . ranges from gruff to antagonistic. He feels that Himmler is spying on him, mistrusts the SS Chief's mythical idolization of the Germanic people and doubts his military capabilities. After the assassination attempt in . . . 1939, Hitler considers himself the victim of a plot, behind which he also suspects Himmler, and threatens, 'This duplicitous animal breeder with his drive for power still has a lot to learn from me.'" In another context he writes, "[Himmler] is living in another world. . . . I'm beginning to think he's out of his head." Following the invasion of Poland: "Hitler notes in his diary that he gave Himmler strict instructions not to carry out any reprisals against the Polish population. The merciless treatment of Polish civilians under the German occupation — an instance of high-handedness by subordinates — [is] a macabre confirmation of the popular saying, 'If the Fuehrer only knew about that.'" Whether through conscious effort or subconscious ideological belief, Hitler's instigation of the atrocities of the Third Reich was at least partly shifted to his fanatical supporters.

Another series of tests — forensic tests conducted by the Bundesarchiv laboratories — were undertaken, and again the examination that clearly should have debunked the diaries failed to do so. The Bundesarchiv laboratory examined a

186 Two pages from the article in *Newsweek* (May 16, 1983) on uncovering the forged diaries

number of the letters purported to have been found with the diaries, as well as various pages from the diaries themselves, and concluded that all of the separate letters were forgeries on the basis of a whitener found in the paper which was not in use until after the war. The Bundesarchiv report seriously questioned the authenticity of the diaries — if they came from the same source. *Stern*, for its part, followed what for them was a logical pattern — Heidemann was asked to investigate this definitive statement that the letters were forgeries. He, of course, called Kujau, who simply stated that the Bundesarchiv was wrong, that the whitener in the paper had been invented in the earlier part of the twentieth century, and that they did not know what they were talking about. Heidemann naturally reported back to *Stern* that there was no cause for concern. *Stern*'s own internal investigation of the whole affair stated that this report did not go beyond Heidemann and Walde; however, Peter Koch personally told me about this forensic examination at the time I was examining the diaries.

Satisfied that they could defend the diaries' authenticity, *Stern* prepared a memorandum discussing provenance for the potential purchasers of publication rights. In the memorandum, thirty-two pages are devoted to the history of the diaries. The first twenty-eight pages discuss the extensive search for the plane crash site, and then, in just a few brief paragraphs, Heidemann's story leaps from the discovery of the crash site to the existence of Hitler's diaries. Having meticulously traced the investigation of the airplane's route, passengers, cargo, and fate, *Stern*'s memorandum continues, "Heidemann gets a few tips about who [might] possess materials from the crashed aircraft. Months later he is successful." There follows a list of Hitler medals, drawings, and other personal items mentioned earlier. Then the memo states:

187a
Hitler's genuine signature

187b
Kujau's much larger forged version, which has a faulty crossbar in addition

> For months, Heidemann searches in the German Democratic Republic, in the Federal Republic of Germany, and among former Nazis such as former SS officer Klaus Altmann, alias Barbie, in South America, in order to find out what else could have been in the aircraft. Most of the information takes him no further. But then comes a tip which interests him. There is talk of a metal chest which might have contained many little composition books inscribed "Property of the Führer" — according to the contents, private note-books. At first, Heidemann doesn't believe that, because no one can show him one of these books. But then the evidence piles up. There may have been at least fifty books . . . on the seal, the imperial eagle with the swastika. . . . The tips were correct.

The books exist. First they are hidden in the vicinity of the crash site, then placed in safe-keeping by a German officer. Those who found them, so it turns out, were aware of the value of the volumes. Nevertheless, the books were held back for a long time, out of fear, out of lack of knowledge about the right way to a historical evaluation. *Stern* is not allowed to reveal the names of those who in April 1945 salvaged Hitler's diaries, when they were hidden or how they got to the West. The earlier owner made it a condition that their anonymity remain preserved.

This initial explanation of the discovery of the diaries was not acceptable to the potential buyers, and *Stern* then advised *Newsweek* that they were coming from a source in East Germany who would be endangered if identified. In interviews immediately after the release of the story, Heidemann stated that in pursuing the diaries, he had visited Austria, Switzerland, Spain, and South America where he met with several exiled Nazis, including Klaus Barbie. "I was startled that nobody had tried to look for [the diaries] before. All it took was a few telephone calls and a few meetings with old Nazis, and the rest was easy." No other information would be provided by Heidemann or *Stern*.

It certainly seemed like a plausible story: the well-documented flight from Berlin of personnel and cargo bound for the Obersalzberg, Hitler's outburst at the loss of the plane, Heidemann's extensive investigation leading to the previously unlocated crash site, his efforts to locate the diaries he heard about, and, veiled in the mysterious world of exiled Nazis and Communist East Germany, the discovery and acquisition of the diaries themselves. It was convincing enough for major news organizations to be bidding millions of dollars for their publication.

Newsweek's cautious confidence in the diaries' authenticity certainly appeared to be well founded. It was reasonable to assume that *Stern* would have investigated every aspect of the "literary property" they were offering at $3.5 million. The atmosphere in the office of the editor, Maynard Parker, when I first met with him, certainly reflected this. Parker had been to Zurich and Hamburg several times to see the diaries and negotiate publication rights. Four days earlier he had been in Zurich with Professor Gerhard Weinberg, whom *Newsweek* had hired as a consultant. While Weinberg was somewhat cautious in his report to Parker, which I was shown that morning, it was clear that he believed the diaries were likely to be authentic. In his published report in the first issue of *Newsweek* concerning the diaries, he accurately identified the problem of *Stern* having had only three pages authenticated, and noted that this in itself did not prove the diaries genuine or fake. Like the other historians who would become involved as the story unfolded, Weinberg, however, speculated outside his field of expertise: "The notion of anyone forging volumes and volumes of diaries seemed very unlikely. The idea of forging hundreds, even thousands of pages of handwriting was hard to credit. One of the unusually striking things was that on almost every page Hitler had signed his name at the bottom. A signature is one thing that can be checked with certainty. It seemed very implausible that anyone forging handwriting would forge gratuitously the one aspect of the handwriting that is most easy to check." He added later, "There is still room — however unlikely — for suspecting that the whole thing is a hoax." Weinberg's decision to consider not only the historical text of the diaries, the area of his expertise, in which he failed, but also to deal with the physical questions of authenticity is difficult to understand. He would, unfortunately, be joined by many other historians in coming weeks.

Despite this air of confidence and an atmosphere of great excitement as *Newsweek* prepared to publish one of the great stories of the postwar era, Parker wanted the most thorough and complete examination of the diaries possible. His confidence in the story, which was shrouded in great secrecy at *Newsweek*, seemed undiminished as I pointed out that there was no evidence that the diaries were genuine or fake. He listened intently as I described how the diaries could be faked and also why it was not at all suspicious for them to be coming to light forty years later. We discussed in some detail the type of examination that would conclusively prove the diaries genuine or fake. This was precisely the approach that *Newsweek* wanted, and they were willing to give me sufficient time and resources to accomplish it.

I was, however, quite concerned that the Hitler diaries story, without any proven basis, had taken on a life of its own; it seemed as though "the train was rolling," as though the historians being consulted were so overawed by the apparent importance of the story that they were not considering the diaries with the same scrutiny they would if in an academic setting. It might be difficult for people in the news media to appreciate how alluring the spotlight of the news is, that suddenly being transported from the academic world to that of interviews in national publications and on network television news might result in focusing on the established story rather than on the basis of the story. People were not questioning the authenticity, only discussing the importance.

Newsweek had stipulated to *Stern* that their own expert would have to examine the complete Hitler "archive" as part of the agreement to purchase publication rights. *Stern* had no objection to this, and I was to spend much of the coming week in Zurich investigating and examining the diaries and other pages. Publication was scheduled for the first of May, two weeks after my initial meeting at *Newsweek*. Time was a consideration, but not a problem.

There was no doubt in my mind that the question of the diaries' authenticity would be resolved within the coming week. But, as at almost every other critical juncture in this saga, the hoax would continue, not as a result of anything planned by the perpetrator but by the action of one of the victims of the hoax, the *Sunday Times* of London. After two days of delays in negotiating the final details of the agreement, *Newsweek* learned that the *Sunday Times* of London would be publishing excerpts from the diaries four days later, one week ahead of schedule. With only a few days left before this new publication date it would be impossible for me to examine the diaries; *Newsweek* would treat the diaries as a news story and report it as such. My role as *Newsweek*'s consultant appeared at an end.

The reaction of the media to the release of *Newsweek*'s Hitler diaries issue was staggering. During the two previous days the Murdoch papers had been bannering the discovery of the diaries and quoting from them, but *Newsweek*'s treatment of the story gave considerable weight to the probability that they were genuine. *Newsweek*'s coverage consisted of twenty-four columns discussing the diaries' text and provenance and only five devoted to "Are They Genuine?" and three to Weinberg's "A Scholar's Appraisal." The magazine certainly noted the possibility that they were not genuine, but the significantly greater emphasis on the content of the diaries rather than their integrity would lead to considerable criticism in the aftermath of the hoax. Television ads showing *Newsweek*'s cover did not include "Are They Genuine?" as did the final cover, and many assumed that *Newsweek* was convinced the diaries were authentic.

The attacks on the diaries' authenticity were immediate and generally misinformed. I had naively believed that once the existence of the diaries was revealed, *Stern* would be compelled to make them available to competent experts to authenticate them definitively. I expected the thrust of the media coverage to focus on the fact that the diaries themselves had never been thoroughly examined and that until they were, the story would focus on *Stern*'s responsibility to do this. I was wrong.

The opportunity to be interviewed on national television and in national publications was too appealing for the many historians and others to resist. The media had little, if any, interest in interviewing anyone who thought there was no story until the diaries were proven genuine. As a result, the historians interviewed discussed the importance of the discovery, not the possibility it was a fraud. The media circus was symbolically established at *Stern*'s first press conference. The conference itself featured two respected historians shouting at each other, with one physically ejected. Trevor-Roper was a featured expert, and he praised the diaries' importance.

Before the conference opened, Heidemann had assured his editors that Martin Bormann had promised to show up and identify the handwriting in the diaries as being that of his former boss. After this news conference, Trevor-Roper learned of Heidemann's outrageous statement about Bormann and it led Trevor-Roper to conclude that Heidemann was crazy. To the historian's credit, he later retracted his press conference comments, stating that he had relied heavily on the provenance described by Heidemann as well as on the authenticity reports and he could no longer be confident in the former. Why did Koch and the other editors not arrive at this entirely reasonable conclusion? Apparently, and appropriately for the subject matter involved, they were blindly following orders from their managing director.

Peter Koch, the editor-in-chief of *Stern*, arrived in New York one week after the first news of the diaries' discovery. He had brought the first and last volumes with him and met with *Newsweek* editors who attempted to negotiate a deal whereby I would be allowed to examine the diaries. The relationship between the two magazines had chilled considerably as Koch accused *Newsweek* of unethically breaking an agreement not to reveal the information given to Parker and Weinberg during negotiations. Koch wanted no further dealings with *Newsweek*. The opportunity to examine the diaries and end the hoax had once again been postponed.

CBS News invited Koch and Rudolph Hess's son, Wolf, who was publicizing his father's fate in Spandau prison by stating that he could authenticate the diaries, to appear on the CBS "Morning News." In discussing the format, it was suggested by CBS that Koch should meet with me, which he agreed to. In a telephone conversation he and I discussed the deplorable situation over the question of authenticity and agreed to meet at CBS studios. It was on the set of the CBS "Morning News" that I first saw the diaries; I went through them with Diane Sawyer and pointed out many factors that proved they were false. To repeat this quick analysis to Koch

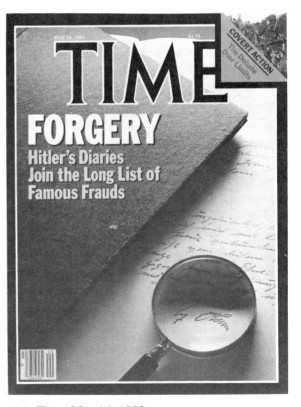

188 *Time*, May 16, 1983

would have resulted in his dismissal of me and my only opportunity to finally put an end to the hoax.

Peter Koch's interview with Diane Sawyer was very impressive. He believed with absolute sincerity that there was no possibility the diaries were forgeries. He told her that he could see no reason for further examinations because three experts had proclaimed them genuine and the testimony of any one of these experts in a criminal case would be sufficient grounds for conviction. During a lengthy breakfast after leaving CBS I realized Koch would never be convinced without overwhelming physical evidence and I therefore avoided discussing the diaries. The invitation to analyze the diaries was largely a result of camaraderie that had developed during a two-hour discussion of ski racing and helicopter skiing; we shared many mutual friends and experiences in the ski world. The Hitler diaries hoax that had begun and was perpetuated by decisions based on personal rather than journalistic considerations was finally beginning to unravel, not because Koch thought the diaries should be thoroughly examined but because he could not see any harm in letting a fellow skier go over them. It was personally flattering but instantly illustrative of how the story had gone so far.

I was now given complete access to the two volumes of diaries, allowed to photocopy them and spend as much time as I wanted at *Stern*'s New York office examining them. Koch was absolutely certain of the outcome of my work. He asked me to be interviewed on a German radio program the next morning, an invitation I knew would be inappropriate. He then departed for an afternoon of shopping at F•A•O Schwarz and other stores. I suggested meeting with him that evening but he would be at a Broadway play. Frank Müller-May, who had accompanied Koch from Hamburg, treated my examination more seriously and followed it very carefully. I showed him the enormous discrepancies in general writing habits, the complete impossibility that Hitler had written the 1945 volume, and a careful analysis of letter patterns to illustrate without question that the 1932 volume was also forged. We discussed how this had gone so far and the importance of locating any records within *Stern* relevant to the origin of the forgeries that were shown to their original three experts. Thomas Walde was called in the middle of the night in Hamburg and went to *Stern*'s office to locate any files relating to these pieces. I departed from *Stern*'s New York office at ten that evening, and we met again at midnight for a late dinner. By then Müller-May told me the third issue on the diaries had been stopped and an international investigation begun.

Koch had been located and would meet with me in the morning.

I did not look forward to meeting with Koch. He had been very trusting in letting me examine the diaries, but I realized it was the same trust, based on personal considerations, that had led him to accept without question the diaries' authenticity. I had been told that he would be forced to resign as a result of the coming scandal, and his physical reaction to the evidence I laid out on a conference table was shocking. I later described him in *Newsweek* as "stunned." Müller-May writing in *Stern* several weeks later recalled, "After only a short look, Peter Koch turned as pale as the paint on the wall." His only question was how the diaries had passed the tests of the three experts who compared them to the Federal Archives examples. It was very evident he had never read the experts' reports. He telephoned Shulte-Hillen, chairman of Gruner und Jahr, and it was agreed that I would go to Hamburg to examine all the materials bought by Heidemann and to provide an independent analysis of how the magazine had been defrauded. Two days later the Bundesarchiv announced that they had conducted further forensic tests on the paper and adhesives as well as researched the texts of the diaries and had conclusive proof they were forgeries.

The Hitler diaries hoax had finally come to an end after two years. The condemnation of *Stern* by journalists throughout the world was no less immediate or severe than that by its own staff members, few of whom were ever involved in the story. In its mea culpa issue they criticized "the higher-ups at the publisher's and in the editorial offices" for failing to have the diaries properly examined for two years. They attributed this to "an exaggerated secrecy and fear for the exclusiveness of their 'superscoop.'" They continued, "The 'biggest journalistic scoop in post-war history' had become even bigger than the few people in on it had ever hoped in their fondest dreams. It was one of the biggest journalistic blunders of all times. In their blatant presentation of Heidemann's hoax, the people responsible had correctly predicted a sensation à la Watergate. Unfortunately it was a Watergate for St*ern*."

Stern's investigation quickly led to Kujau. The later trial of Heidemann and Kujau never determined whether Heidemann was a willing participant in the fraud or a fool who sincerely believed the diaries genuine. In either case, he was guilty of defrauding *Stern* of the money he claimed to have paid Kujau but in fact kept for himself. Kujau turned the trial into a circus, openly admitting his guilt and signing Hitler autographs for spectators. Both received prison terms of four and a half years.

8

The Mormon Forger,
Con Man, and Murderer

189 Kenneth Rendell, with the White Salamander letter in hand, testifying at the trial of Mark Hofmann

The Mormon bombing, forgery, and fraud case is one of incredible complexity. As one of the most famous forgery cases of the twentieth century, it has much in common with the Hitler diaries fraud, notably making the victims want the forgeries to be genuine. The Mormon forger, however, was much more skilled in every aspect of the creation of his forgeries and fraud and the results of the hoax far more devastating on a personal level. With the Hitler diaries the victims lost their careers; in the Mormon case two persons lost their lives.

Mark Hofmann, a disillusioned Mormon and local part-time dealer in historical documents in Salt Lake City, forged documents of major significance to Mormon history, some of which involved rewriting the early history of the founding of the church. He was able to sell most of these documents to the Mormon Church itself and others to Mormons interested in collecting documents relating to Mormon history. Hofmann also created forgeries of printed pieces that caused great controversy among experts until he admitted creating them. In addition, he sold interests in a fictitious Mormon collection, the McLellin Papers, to many different individuals, until he had sold the collection five or six times over. Hofmann reaped hundreds of thousands of dollars from his forgeries and frauds and might have sold one printed piece, the "Oath of a Freeman," for over a million dollars had the McLellin Papers fraud not unraveled. The discovery of that fraud necessitated, in his mind, the killing of three people.

Hofmann was a master at gaining the confidence of his victims. Even after he was charged with murder, virtually everyone who knew him could not believe him guilty. It was inconceivable to me that he could have been the bomber. While I did not know Hofmann as well as his victims, my five or six encounters with him left me with the clear opinion that he could not have been a murderer. I realize, of course, that I had no idea what a murderer would be like; it is quite frightening to realize that a person who appears to be normal is in fact capable of cold-blooded murders.

Hofmann's expertise in forging letters and documents was founded upon an unprecedented amount of research into the historical content of the forged pieces, ensuring that historians could not fault the texts he created. His scientific approach to the forgeries themselves was also unprecedented. He created copper plates from genuine postmarks and printed them on address leaves with ink that he made to exacting contemporary formulas, using ingredients obtained from natural sources, including burning contemporary paper to obtain carbon; he

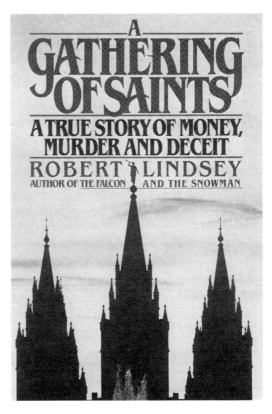

190 An account of Mark Hofmann's forgery career and criminal activities as told by Robert Lindsey in *A Gathering of Saints: A True Story of Money, Murder and Deceit*

added seals to letters by scraping the original wax seals off genuine letters of the correct period and reheating the wax for use on the forgery; and he created embossed seals through an electroplating process based on genuine examples. Yet, despite all this effort, every forged letter and document, with one exception, was uncovered and scientifically proven false when examined under ultraviolet light.

For his forgeries of printing, Hofmann relied on a different method for aging and oxidizing the ink, a method that did not result in the scientific evidence of forgery that was found when his letters and documents were examined under ultraviolet light. His forgery of the "Oath of a Freeman," believed to be the first piece of printing in America, went undetected (though it was highly suspect) until he confessed to its creation and explained his methods.

I first met Mark Hofmann sometime in the late 1970s. He was an introverted person, someone one could never really get to know, but a person who appeared to be a serious collector, Mormon scholar, and part-time dealer in Mormon historical material. He was all of these things, but beneath this surface, he was also beginning to experiment with forging letters of great importance to Mormon history.

Hofmann later testified that he had become disillusioned with the Mormon religion when he was fourteen years old and that the forgeries he created were based on what he believed had actually happened in Mormon history rather than on what the church claimed. For example, he believed the church was based on magic spells in which Joseph Smith was involved, and he therefore created the text of the so-called White Salamander letter as a more likely and reasonable description of the finding of the golden plates than the church's official version. (According to the Mormon religion these plates contained, in addition to the Old and New Testaments, an entirely new book of scriptures.) He believed that by thoroughly knowing the Mormon Church's official version of its history and creating letters and documents that contained historical versions of these events in keeping with what many people thought actually did happen, he could get away with his frauds.

The first two or three forgeries created by Hofmann did not seriously challenge any teachings of the church, and he planned his "discoveries" of these documents exceptionally well. Beyond the content of the letters, their provenance was meticulously planned; every detail had to be logical and verifiable. Representing himself as a believing member of the Mormon Church, he always portrayed his interests as protecting the history of the church, and he was seen in many newspaper photographs with the leaders of the Mormon Church and his important "discoveries."

Hofmann also later testified that he always represented himself as an amateur, allowing church historians to tell him the importance of what he had found, never betraying his own extensive and detailed knowledge. Illustrative of this technique was the way in which Mark Hofmann brought to light his forgery of the Anthon Transcript.

Hofmann brought a copy of a 1668 Cambridge edition of the King James Bible to the curator of the Utah State University rare book library and explained to him that he had acquired the Bible because it was signed by Samuel Smith. Hofmann hoped that this would turn out to be an ancestor of Joseph Smith. On further examining the Bible, Hofmann found that two pages had been glued together and he asked for the curator's assistance in finding a conservator to separate the pages. As the pages were separated, a manuscript in hieroglyphic characters was found pasted between them, a manuscript that would be identified by the curator and authenticated by Mormon Church historians as one of the most important discoveries in Mormon history. Hofmann, who professed to having bought the book only because of its potential connection to Joseph Smith's family, appeared dumbfounded at the tremendous discovery made by the curator and while meeting with the leaders of the church, told them that he of course wanted it to remain forever in the church's archives. The manuscript, as later shown, was a forgery by Hofmann, and the entire scheme of letting the curator discover it and become the proponent of its authenticity would become a Hofmann trademark.

When Hofmann decided to become more daring in testing his skills, he forged a letter of the Mormon prophet, Joseph Smith. In knowing that this creation would undergo more scrutiny because there would be known handwriting with which to compare it, he decided to preempt investigators. He took the letter himself to a noted New York City auctioneer and expert and asked him if it was genuine. This auctioneer knew Hofmann in the same context that I did — as someone always looking for Mormon material — so it would not be surprising to have him turn up with a Joseph Smith letter for authentication. Unfortunately, after a cursory examination the auctioneer wrote a statement of authenticity. This gave Hofmann an even greater sense of self-confidence and allowed him to sell the forged Joseph Smith letter readily in the Salt Lake City market.

No small part of Hofmann's confidence was based on the unprecedented scientific foundation of his forgeries. His skill at imitating handwriting was very good, but it is in the manufacture of the correct ink of the period that he had no equal. In addition to creating the right formula, the forger must oxidize the ink and prevent it from feathering out into the older paper. Hofmann used two chemicals to accomplish this, hydrogen peroxide and ammonia hydrochloride. These created exactly what he wanted — ink with the appearance of age and with an absorption into the paper consistent with what one would see in examining letters of this period. This aging process did, however, produce two other effects that he did not anticipate; one of these, the fact that either of these chemicals can cause paper to fluoresce a bright blue under high-intensity ultraviolet light, was the scientific proof that unmasked his years of work in less than half an hour.

Sometime in 1983, according to Hofmann, he decided to create his boldest forgery, the so-called White Salamander letter, which cast doubt on Joseph Smith's version of the finding of the golden plates. Great effort went into the creation of this letter. The text was researched in such depth that the reference in the first line to the writer receiving a letter the previous day was verified by checking postal schedules. The physical preparation was even more thorough than for the other forgeries. Hofmann did not have to worry about imitating handwriting in this case because no hand-writing of the author of the White Salamander letter was known except for a few signatures — not enough to base a comparison on. The postmark and wax were genuine; Hofmann had acquired a perfectly genuine letter of the correct period and wrote the White Salamander letter on the back of the address leaf, a not uncommon practice at that time. He later stated that he aged the paper even more by exposing it to bread mold that he grew himself. This letter is by far his best forgery because unlike all the others, it does not give off a bluish tint when examined under ultraviolet light.

The fact that the Salamander letter does not match the other forgeries in this regard has raised a number of interesting questions. Hofmann himself, in his posttrial testimony, could not explain how he created the White Salamander letter without the bluish tint. Of all the forgeries, it is the most damaging to the Mormon's claims about its history and is the one Hofmann discovery the church was most anxious to discredit. George Throckmorton, a Salt Lake City ques-tioned document expert who is a member of the Mormon Church, had told me that he had been able to create in his laboratory the same effect that Hofmann did — a clear and strong pen line without the feathering of the ink into the paper and without the bluish tint. In a visit to his laboratory in Salt Lake City with the assistant prosecutor in the case, Mr. Throckmorton was unable to demonstrate his claim. The probability that Hofmann forged the White Salamander letter was overwhelming, but the lack of the bluish tint in only this forgery was quite curious.

The importance of the White Salamander letter lies in the doubt it casts on the credibility of the church founder, Joseph Smith. According to the official version of the church's founding, Smith was led by an angel of God to a hidden cache of gold plates which contained a third volume of scripture as well as the Old and New Testaments. This third volume is the Book of Mormon, which forms the basis of the Mormon religion. The White Salamander letter, however, presents a different version. Martin Harris, the writer of the letter and friend of Smith's, quotes him as saying that he was led to the plates by a spirit, which transfigured itself into a white salamander and struck him. The salamander is a familiar folk magic symbol. The implication is that Smith was a dabbler in folk magic and the occult and not a religious prophet.

Late in 1983, Hofmann asked me to examine the Salamander letter and tell him what I thought of it. There was no known genuine handwriting of the purported author of the White Salamander letter, Martin Harris, except for the few signatures that would be insufficient to establish authenticity. Thus, with no available source of handwriting for comparison, I could only examine the handwriting for evidence of the usual characteristics of inconsistency found in forgeries and to verify the type of postmark and the other characteristics that would be found in a genuine letter of the period. The content could not be verified because of its controversial nature, but Hofmann's story of the history of the letter was verified and the provenance was found to be logical: he had acquired the letter from a dealer in stampless covers who also happened to be a Mormon; this individual had bought it from another dealer in stampless covers in New Hampshire who had sold it only for its postal value — he had never unfolded the letter to read it. After buying it for its postal value, Hofmann's source then read the letter and realized its importance. With the provenance verified by questioning these two dealers and with no evidence of forgery in the handwriting or other unusual characteristics (it fluoresced normally under high-powered ultraviolet light), I informed Hofmann, "I found no evidence of forgery, which is not to say it is genuine."

Hofmann then had the letter examined by an ink specialist and a paper specialist who both wrote reports stating that there was nothing inconsistent in the materials with the date on the letter. The Federal Bureau of Investigation later did an exhaustive analysis of the White Salamander letter, and their report concluded, "Although lack of sufficient known signatures and writing prevented a definitive conclusion, similarities were observed which indicate these writings were probably written by the same person. . . . These writings appear to have been normally written and no evidence was observed which would indicate forgery or an attempt to copy or simulate the writing of another. . . . There is no evidence to suggest that these documents were prepared at a time other than their reported dates."

When news of the discovery of the White Salamander letter was released in the media, there was little interest outside of the Mormon Church faithful. And even in these circles, I was told, many believed that the story told by Harris was what really happened — that Joseph Smith was involved with folk magic and had invented the story of the angel.

A very important part of Hofmann's scheme involving the White Salamander letter was the provenance. In the absence of any indication of forgery in the letter itself, there was also no evidence that it was genuine, but the story Hofmann had created was virtually foolproof. Before the advent of postage stamps, letters were written on double sheets of 8-1/2 by 10-inch paper. The second sheet was folded in such a way as to become the envelope for the letter. On this second sheet, post offices applied their postmarks and notations as to payment for transmittal in the postal system. Dealers in these so-called stampless covers are only interested in the postmarks, not the content of the letters inside, and it was not at all unusual that a dealer specializing in stampless covers had sold one without opening it (after all, he could spend his lifetime reading routine family letters and never discover anything of any importance). The dealer who stated that he originally sold the White Salamander letter remembered the address panel and postal markings — which were exactly as they were when he had sold them. Hofmann had removed the integral leaf containing the original letter and had written the White Salamander letter on the back of sheet containing the address panel. The dealer was correct in verifying that he had sold the piece, but when he sold it, the letter was not written on it. Hofmann told me that the White Salamander letter had been discovered by Lyn Jacobs, a dealer in Mormon memorabilia and stampless covers who confirmed this to me, and the dealer in New Hampshire stated that he had sold the stampless cover to Lyn Jacobs. It was all very logical.

At about the same time that the White Salamander letter was making news, Hofmann was involved in creating another ingenious forgery that apparently was part of what many later concluded was his master plan for rewriting Mormon Church history. The Deseret Book Company in Salt Lake City, owned by the Mormon Church, had a rare book department, and in the vault of that department there was a copy of the Book of Common Prayer which had been signed by someone named Nathan Harris. The manager of the rare book department suggested to Hofmann that this might be Martin Harris's brother, one of Joseph Smith's early followers and the purported writer of the White Salamander letter. Hofmann bought the book for fifty dollars.

A few days later, he returned to the store, stating that he had found a short poem in the rear flyleaf of the book which had, in fact, been written by Martin Harris himself, and he felt that the Deseret Book Company was entitled to a much higher price for the book. He told the manager that he had in fact sold the book with these notes by Martin Harris to the Mormon Church for two thousand dollars and he thought it only fair that he pay the Deseret Book Company an additional thousand dollars.

The importance of this transaction was not in the money that it netted Hofmann — one thousand dollars — but in establishing another example of Martin Harris's handwriting. When Hofmann purchased the book from the Deseret Book Company, Harris's notes were not in the book. These he added after purchasing it. But with a book of relatively small value, it was entirely reasonable that a series of notes would have gone unnoticed. The dealer thought Hofmann was being unbelievably generous, while Hofmann was, in fact, establishing the basis for an even greater fraud.

Many believe that this larger fraud was to have been perpetrated after the McLellin Collection fraud, which caused Hofmann's overall scheme to be discovered. The fraud was based on the fact that Martin Harris, as Joseph Smith's scribe, had written one hundred sixteen pages of the Book of Mormon. These pages were then lost and have been, understandably, of great interest to the Mormon Church. The church had based its claim to be God's only true church on the literal truth of the Book of Mormon and Joseph Smith's account of its discovery; the one hundred sixteen pages were therefore critical to its legitimacy.

Having established examples of Martin Harris's handwriting, Hofmann would then be in a position to "discover" the missing one hundred sixteen pages and could have created any text that he wanted. He once told a collector in Provo, Utah, that if he found the missing pages, he could get ten million dollars for them. He thought there was no question of having an immediate buyer in the Mormon Church — whatever the content of the missing pages. He could write a text promoting the history of the church as they told it or he could create a text that would cause the church's fundamental theology to lose its credibility. In the latter case, he could possibly have sold the manuscript to those who would suppress its text and then through some devious means, release its content to the public. Whatever the scenario, Mark Hofmann was establishing Martin Harris's handwriting for some purpose far beyond a small financial profit.

Hofmann next turned his attention to forging printed pieces. One excellent example was the missing page of a rare Mormon book, expertly printed and inserted by Hofmann, thereby increasing the value of the book by thousands of dollars (this forged addition was made even more believable by creating a water stain on the newly inserted page to match the one on the preceding page, indicating that water had run from one page to the other many years before).

Hofmann also forged other printed pieces, including receipt forms to which he added signatures, notably the Confederate raider Quantrill, and the mountain man, Jim Bridger (signed with an X) [191], as well as extensive runs of Mormon currency (many of these were previously unknown and were included in a new edition of the standard reference book on Mormon currency). In addition, he began forging inscriptions in books.

No Hofmann forgery could have had the impact on the world of rare books as his next forgery, that of the first piece of printing in America, the "Oath of a Freeman," of which no example has survived. His provenance for this piece was as ingenious as any of his manuscript forgery frauds. He first printed a broadside entitled "Oath of a Freeman," forged a price of twenty-five dollars on the verso, in the same manner as that of a New York City bookseller who offers such miscellaneous broadsides for sale in large boxes for people to search through. Having placed his own crude forgery in the dealer's box, he then purchased it and obtained a receipt for a broadside entitled, "Oath of a Freeman." Any knowledgeable person would believe that it could be possible that a large bookseller could miss the importance of such a piece and put it with routine broadsides. Hofmann had his provenance and then set out to create his forgery.

The paper was obtained in his usual manner — he stole blank pages of contemporary books from collections of rare books at local university libraries — and he made his own ink. He had obtained extensive knowledge of the manufacture of printing inks and had even burned contemporary paper to

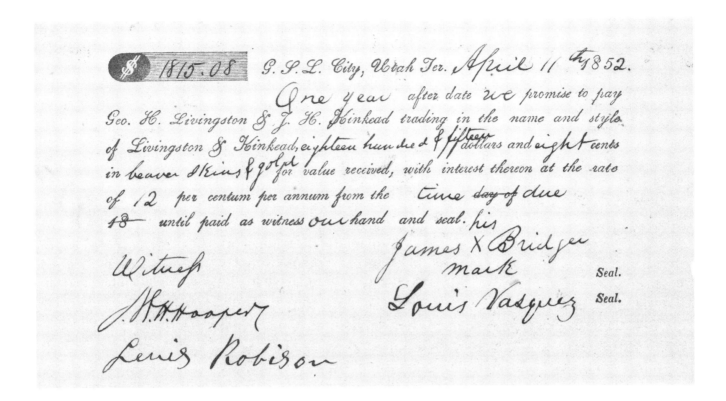

create the carbon for use in making the ink. He was extremely meticulous in ensuring that the components of the ink could not be dated as recent. The major difference in this and his manuscript forgeries was in the use of ozone in oxidizing the ink and preventing its feathering into the paper. Unknown to Hofmann, this process did not cause the blue fluorescence that was so quickly identified in his forgeries of letters and documents. Ozone must be used as it is being made; it cannot be stored and is therefore more difficult to use. The forging of the printing itself is outside my area of expertise, and I refer the reader to *Fakes and Frauds: Varieties of Deception in Print and Manuscript*, which contains an excellent article by Nicholas Barker on the "Oath of a Freeman."

The "Oath of a Freeman" was offered for sale by Hofmann at $1.5 million and it was seriously considered by the Library of Congress and the American Antiquarian Society. Their experts could not fault its authenticity, although many did not believe it genuine for what were various nonscientific reasons.

In the summer of 1985, Hofmann expected to complete his sale of the "Oath of a Freeman" and in anticipation of this income, began making commitments to pay for rare books and other objects he was purchasing. Throughout the summer, the financial pressure increased as the sale was still

191 A forgery of a partly printed receipt with the signature, *X*, of the mountain Jim Bridger, by Mark Hofmann. Both the printing and handwriting were forged by Hofmann

pending and his creditors demanded payment. It was under this pressure that Hofmann created a fictitious collection, the McLellin Papers.

Hofmann claimed that the McLellin Papers contained manuscripts of the greatest importance to Mormon history, but as he later admitted, he told as many different stories about the content of the collection as the number of people he sold it to. He not only sold this nonexistent collection several times over but also sold percentages of interest in it to those who could not afford to purchase the whole collection; eventually, these part ownerships totaled many times over 100 percent.

By the end of the summer of 1985, Hofmann decided he had to come up with some proof of the existence of the McLellin Papers and he obtained from me, on consignment, two large pieces of a second century A.D. Egyptian Book of the Dead, written on papyrus, containing many drawings and a text from the Book of the Dead [192, 193]. He cut up one of these and showed the pieces to the investors and purchasers of the McLellin Papers. He told them that the papyri pieces were from that collection and that they were from the earliest period of Mormon history.

The significance of the papyri manuscripts and their dating related to the existence, at one time, of the papers of the early Mormon apostle, William McLellin. That collection was said to contain papyri fragments that were translated by Joseph Smith into the Book of Abraham. There had been no trace of the whereabouts of William McLellin's papers, and Mark Hofmann's claim to have discovered them, complete with the original Egyptian manuscripts which Joseph Smith had translated, created enormous interest among Mormons.

The upper left corner of one of the pieces Hofmann obtained from me was mounted by Hofmann on a backing with markings similar to those on the papyri fragments known to have come directly from Joseph Smith [194]. That group from Joseph Smith was later obtained by the Metropolitan Museum of Art in New York, which donated them to the Mormon Church in 1967. The Metropolitan had dated these pieces of papyri at A.D. 60.

The upper left corner of my Book of the Dead, mounted like the Joseph Smith pieces, was later found in the safe deposit box of Steve Christensen, a Mormon businessman who was interested in church history. He had purchased the Salamander letter through Mark Hofmann. Christensen had also been involved in arranging a loan to Mark Hofmann from the Mormon Church for $180,000 to enable him to

192 One of the two pieces of papyri from the Egyptian Book of the Dead which Hofmann had on approval from Kenneth W. Rendell and which he represented as being from Joseph Smith. Its plexiglass encapsulation is heavily scarred and burned by the bomb that nearly killed Hofmann.

193
A fragment of the second piece of the Book of the Dead found in the vault of Hofmann's first bombing victim, Steve Christensen

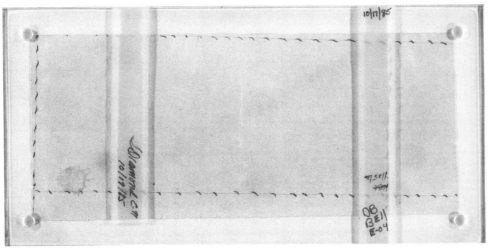

194
The verso of the above papyrus, showing the markings Hofmann had added, which are similar to those on papyri fragments known to have come directly from Joseph Smith

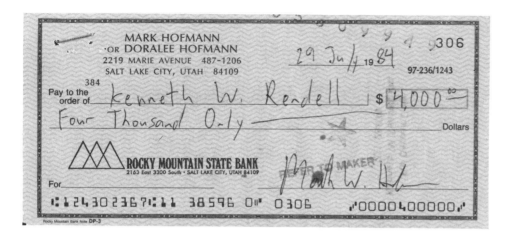

195
A rare example of Hofmann's own handwriting — in the form of an unpaid check

purchase the McLellin Papers. When Christensen heard from others that they too had bought the McLellin Papers, he immediately demanded repayment of the church's loan, accused him of double-dealing, and threatened to both expose Hofmann and have him arrested if he did not either deliver the collection or repay the $180,000 immediately.

At this time, I telephoned Hofmann asking about the status of the two pieces of papyrus and also letting him know that I would be visiting Salt Lake City in several weeks and wanted to meet with him and other collectors. My upcoming visit greatly increased the pressure on Hofmann. He knew I would be seeing several of the collectors he had not only sold forgeries to but had also shown fragments of my Book of the Dead.

With the pressure from Christensen to either deliver the collection or return the church's money, neither of which he could do, and my impending visit, it was clear that Hofmann was in a desperate situation. He decided to kill Christensen. Hofmann already had a considerable knowledge of explosives, and during the first week of October 1985, he tested various bombs in remote areas. He determined the amount of gunpowder required to kill a person and then wrapped a pipe bomb in nails to further ensure fatal damage. Hofmann's attempts at covering his purchases of the bomb components were not thorough, and he was later rather quickly traced to each of the stores where they were obtained.

Christensen was killed on Monday morning, October 15, and later that day, a bomb that Hofmann had left at the house of Christensen's business partner, Gary Sheets, exploded, killing Sheets's wife. The Sheets bombing was a diversion: Christensen and Sheets were involved in a financial company that was entering bankruptcy and Hofmann wanted to make it appear that disgruntled investors had killed both of them. (The *Wall Street Journal* reported these two bombings in their Tuesday edition as just this.)

Two days later Hofmann himself was seriously injured when a bomb exploded in his car. When he regained consciousness, he told investigators that when he opened his car door a package began to tumble out and then exploded. They knew at that time that they had the bomber, for the physical evidence in the car completely contradicted Hofmann's story and they were certain that he was not a victim but rather that a bomb intended for a third victim had accidentally gone off. (When Hofmann got into his car, he was on his way to meet a collector to whom he had sold a number of forgeries, a collector whom he knew I would be visiting the next week.)

During the following months, the Salt Lake City homicide department and the Salt Lake City county prosecutor's office developed a very strong case against Hofmann as the murderer of Christensen and Sheets, but their greatest challenge was in pursuing the motives for the murders — the documents Hofmann had been selling.

In the months preceding the preliminary trial (in Utah such a proceeding determines if there is probable cause; the defense may cross-examine witnesses and present its own evidence and witnesses), forensic experts hired by the prosecutors found another common denominator among the Hofmann "discoveries" — a cracking of the ink, which when magnified, has the appearance of a reptile's skin [196]. They determined that the chemicals used (hydrogen peroxide or ammonia hydrochloride) had been applied over an iron base galotannic ink to which gum arabic had been added for thickening and that the reaction of the two raised the pH of the ink, causing it to coagulate and crack. This cracking is unnoticeable unless one is looking for it and completely unremarkable except as a common denominator among the Hofmann forgeries.

On January 31, 1986, I was visited by the principal investigators and the prosecutor. They showed me approximately twenty-five manuscript pieces as well as some printed pieces, indicating they believed several of these were forgeries. After examining the twenty-five pieces for half an hour, I told them that I thought all probably were forgeries. This was based upon easily observable facts — shaky handwriting, and the color and feel of the ink and paper, which indicated they had been artificially aged. A few minutes of a fairly routine examination with a high-powered ultraviolet light revealed that each of the pieces had been coated, almost painted, with a chemical that fluoresced bright blue. Not only were paintbrush strokes visible but you could also see where clips had been applied in the corners to hang the pieces up to dry. One document that was in fact genuine but had a forged section added to it only fluoresced blue in this area. You could

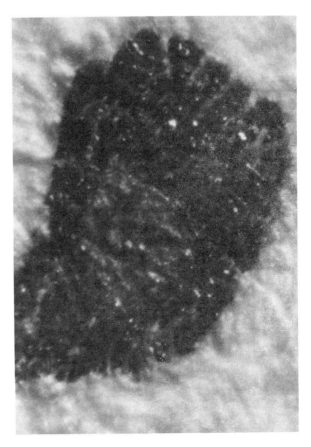

196 An enlargement of one of the characteristics in the writing of Hofmann's forgeries — a cracking of the ink

actually see where the forger had painted the chemical over the lines he had written. It was immediately apparent that this chemical was the agent that had prevented the feathering of the ink into the paper, a characteristic that would normally occur.

Three days later, Hofmann was formally charged with the killings and forgeries. My testimony at the trial concerned the provenance of my Book of the Dead, dealings with Hofmann concerning it, and the twenty-five or so pieces that I had been shown in January [189]. I discussed in detail the bluish tint seen under high-powered ultraviolet light (Hofmann later stated that this was one of the biggest surprises in the trial) and, of course, the authenticity of the Salamander letter. There was still no physical evidence that it was a forgery. It did not have the bluish tint that all the other forgeries had, and the ink and paper experts had not found anything in the materials to indicate that it was not of that date. Questions about the Salamander letter were finally ended when I suggested to the judge that no one was asking me the right question: if someone would ask me if I would buy the letter believing it might be genuine, my answer would be a resounding no!

The evidence against Hofmann was overwhelming on all charges, and in late 1986 he began plea bargaining. There was considerable dissension within the prosecutor's office about negotiations for a plea bargain, as it was widely believed that the state had an overwhelming case against Hofmann and did not need to make any agreements to get a conviction. The only non-Mormon prosecutor on the prosecution team was fired for his protests over making a deal with Hofmann.

When the terms of the plea bargain were announced to the public, the Mormon community and citizens of Utah were outraged. Hofmann had pleaded guilty to two counts of second degree murder — not premeditated — and two counts of forgery, but what the prosecutors thought they had gotten in return was an agreement from Hofmann to answer their questions about the details of his frauds.

Many people close to the case believed that what the prosecution had actually accomplished was to avoid a very embarrassing trial for the Mormon Church. Church officials had been "excused" from having to testify at the preliminary hearing even though their business dealings with Hofmann had been very extensive and even though there were claims that the Mormon Church was interested in buying and suppressing any historical manuscripts that disproved their own version of their founding. With the plea bargain, there would be no scrutiny of the church's dealings with him or questions about what they did with the manuscripts that they did buy. (I was told by a detective who questioned Hofmann after the plea bargain that Hofmann told him that the remainder of my Egyptian Book of the Dead had been sold to the Mormon Church and that, believing it to be from Joseph Smith, they had no intention of it ever seeing the light of day. When the detective made inquiries of the Mormon officials with whom Hofmann was doing business, they declined to discuss the matter.)

Hofmann received the only possible sentence: five years-to-life for second degree murder. In February 1987, at the Utah State Prison, there began a series of interviews with the detectives, prosecutors, and Hofmann. On May 27, these interviews abruptly ended. On that day, Hofmann's attorney, who had successfully blocked numerous questions by stating that Hofmann did not care to discuss them, announced that Hofmann would answer no further questions unless arrangements were made to transfer him to a better cell. Having realized that much of the information they were getting from Hofmann was not accurate and that he was declining to discuss any questions of substance, the prosecutors finally drew the line.

In January 1988, Hofmann received a hearing with the State of Utah Board of Pardons, an entity that would decide what his sentence would be. The Board was chilled by Hofmann's detachment when discussing the murders, saying, "It was almost a game. . . . It didn't matter if it was Mrs. Sheets, a child, a dog . . . whoever was killed." Twenty-seven minutes later, the Board rendered its verdict, stating that they were dismayed by his "callous disregard for human life" and sentenced him to life in prison without parole. Two months later Hofmann approached two different inmates in the prison, stating that he had money hidden outside of the prison and that he would pay them $10,000 each to kill the members of the Board of Pardons.

Hofmann had said at his hearing that deceiving people had given him a sense of power, and it was clear in the interviews that he gave after his guilty plea that he was certainly exercising that power. Everyone closely involved with the events knew that many of Hofmann's answers were lies.

The most tantalizing major question remaining for many people is whether or not Mark Hofmann actually did all of the forgeries himself. The forgeries are of two quite different levels of handwriting skill — some very crude and others extremely well executed — and these two different types were produced at the same time. It was clearly not a case of

Jany the 12th 1803

I Certify that Robert Miller has Don five Days Service as Scout in my District

Daniel Boone

Boston May 10, 1814

Rec'd of John Powell seven dollars in full for one Set Silver Tea Spoons

Paul Revere

197, 198
Two well-executed forgeries by Mark Hofmann
— a document purportedly signed by Daniel
Boone and a receipt of Paul Revere

Hofmann becoming more skilled as time went on: crude forgeries turn up just after a very skillful one (compare Hofmann's own handwriting, 195, with 197 and 198, two reasonably well-executed forgeries). At a meeting in George Throckmorton's laboratory in Salt Lake City before the trial, he and I agreed that if the Salamander letter was a forgery, it almost certainly was done by someone other than the forger of the other pieces.

Perhaps the whole story of Mark Hofmann will never be known. Even if he were to agree to a series of interviews today, or in the future, one would always have to keep in mind that Hofmann's life has been fueled by the power he felt in deceiving people. Facing life imprisonment is now his only challenge.

9

The Jack the Ripper Ripoff

7 OCTOBER 1993

THE DAY THE WORLD'S
GREATEST MURDER MYSTERY
WILL BE SOLVED

The
DIARY
of
JACK
the
RIPPER

THE DISCOVERY
THE INVESTIGATION
THE AUTHENTICATION

"All the bitches will pay. Before
I am finished all England will know
the name I have given myself."

SMITH GRYPHON PUBLISHERS

199 The publicity brochure for *The Diary of Jack the Ripper*, published by Smith Gryphon

The discovery of Jack the Ripper's purported diary was first reported in 1992. My only reaction was curiosity as to what examinations had been done to determine its authenticity. After the Hitler diaries scandal of nearly a decade earlier, I assumed the English publisher, Robert Smith, would be extremely thorough. My personal interest in the activities or identity of Jack the Ripper was minimal at most, and I did not give the subject any further thought until I received a telephone call from Time-Warner the first week of August 1993.

They had bought the United States publication rights from the English publisher in February 1993 and had been requesting since then that they be provided with the diary in order to conduct their own independent investigation of its authenticity. The English publisher, Robert Smith, had told Warner Books that Shirley Harrison needed the original diary until she completed writing the chapters concerned with the purported author's life and the historical background of the murders. This text was finally delivered to Warner in mid-July. Meanwhile Warner had made over 200,000 advance sales to booksellers and was planning to release the U.S. edition on October 7, the date set by the English publisher for worldwide release. (In addition to the United States and England, editions were being published in Canada, Australia, Germany, France, the Netherlands, Spain, Italy, and Japan.) By the first week of August, time was becoming a factor.

My reaction to the telephone call from Warner was twofold — a sense that the publishing world should not be embarassed by another literary hoax (Mussolini's diaries, Howard Hughes's autobiography, and Hitler's diaries had been enough) and also curiosity. Whatever the diary was, genuine or fake, it would be an interesting investigation. Surely, I assumed, the English publisher had had the best experts available examine the diary as thoroughly as possible. In fact, he had even mentioned the Hitler diaries in his promotional literature when describing the process of authentication. His statements about the authentication process were definitive. According to them, all the experts had clearly found it to be genuine.

At a meeting at Warner Books in New York the following day, the chief executive officer, Laurence J. Kirshbaum, and the editor-in-chief, Joann Davis, made it absolutely clear that Warner Books would delay publication if necessary and cancel it if I determined the diary was a forgery. In view of the statements concerning authenticity by the English publisher, it was possible, I told them, that I could neither prove nor demonstrate a definitive conclusion. If there were questions of authenticity but not proof of forgery, Warner would publish the book with my report as a prologue. I left with the page proofs of *The Diary of Jack the Ripper: The Discovery, the Investigation, and the Authentication* to read during the next several days.

As I read the book, I was overwhelmed by the similarities to the Hitler diaries — numerous instances of conclusions not based on the facts presented, an unknown history of the diary (the original discoverer was dead and it took over 100 years for it to be found despite its author writing, "I place this now in a place where it shall be found"), and a clear sense that the author approached the questions of authenticity with little skepticism and a strong inclination toward "positive thinking."

The major difference, however, was that the Hitler diaries could quickly be proven genuine or false because of the amount of genuine handwriting of Hitler that was available for comparison (even though it had not been used) and the enormous body of biographical and historical facts of known accuracy. In the Jack the Ripper case, the situation was more complicated because there was no known positively genuine handwriting of the killer (nor his or her real identity). Of the person purported in the book to be Jack the Ripper, James Maybrick, it was indicated that there was only one genuine signature known, possibly a second. (It was not until later that it became clear that a sufficiently lengthy document, entirely in Maybrick's hand, existed [201].)

My approach to the question of the authenticity of the Jack the Ripper diary was to examine it from every possible standpoint, and I intended to form a group of experts in as many fields as necessary to accomplish this task. Initially, I had only the text of the Harrison book to work with. (Throughout this chapter I refer to the "published text" or "book" to indicate the page proofs I was given. As I pointed out contradictions and errors in the text, many were changed; therefore, some references may not be valid for some published versions of the book.) My examination began with the information provided by the text itself.

The 235-page book, written by Shirley Harrison, describes the alleged discovery of the Jack the Ripper diary by Tony Devereux, who gave the diary to a friend, Mike Barrett, refusing to explain where it came from. (Devereux is now dead; he never mentioned an obviously very valuable diary to his family.) Barrett then researched the diary's contents and determined that the text was written by James Maybrick, a Liverpool cotton merchant. Maybrick had been addicted to arsenic and strychnine, and his young American wife was charged with murdering him after years of marital problems.

The pain is unbearable. My dear Bunny knows all. I do not know if she has the strength to kill me, I pray to God she finds it. It would be simple, she knows of my medicine, and for an extra dose or two it would be all over. No one will know. I have seen to that. George knows of my habit and I trust soon it will come to the attention of Michael. In truth I believe he is aware of the fact. Michael will know how to act, he is the most sensible amongst us all. I do not believe I will see this June, my favourite of all months. Have begged Bunny to act soon, I curse myself for the coward I am. I have redressed the balance of my previous will. Bunny and the children are well cared for and I trust Michael and Thomas will carry out my wishes.

Soon, I trust I shall be laid beside my dear mother and father. I shall seek their forgiveness when we are reunited. God I pray, will allow me at least that privilege, although I know only too well I do not deserve it. My thoughts will remain in tact, for a reminder to all how love does destroy — I place this now in a place were it shall be found. I pray whoever should read this will find it in their heart to forgive me. Remind all, whoever you may be, that I was once a gentle man. May the good lord have mercy on my soul, and forgive me for all I have done.

I give my name that all know of me, so history do tell, what love can do to a gentle man born.

Yours truly

Jack the Ripper

Dated this third day of May 1889.

200 The final page of the forged diary

144

Association of New York both Policies
being made out in her name. The interest
on this £2500. together with the £125 a year
which she receives from her New York property
will make a provision of about £425 a
year, a sum although small will yet be
the means of keeping her respectably.

It is also my desire that my widow shall
live under the same roof with the Children
so long as she remains my widow.

If it is legally possible I wish the £2000
of Life Insurance on my life in my wifes
name to be invested in the names of
the said Trustees, but that she should
have the sole use of the interest thereof
during her lifetime, but at her death the
principal to revert to my said Children
James Chandler & Gladys Evelyn Maybrick.

Witness my hand & seal this
twenty fifth day of April 1889.

Signed by the Testator in the
presence of us who at his
request in his presence
and in the presence of each
other have hereunto affixed
our names as Witnesses

George Davidson.
Geo Smith

James Maybrick

201 James Maybrick's will in his hand and signed by him

145

The Harrison book details Maybrick's life, presumably based on accounts written about Maybrick after his alleged murder in 1889. Having shown that the diary's author was Maybrick and that he had to be Jack the Ripper, the full text of the diary is printed with an analysis by David Forshaw, a psychiatric consultant in addictions. Dr. Forshaw's conclusion is that the diary does indeed reveal the mind of Jack the Ripper. The book concludes with a discussion of the authentication process.

The first outside expert I brought in was Joe Nickell, most noted for his work and book concerning the Shroud of Turin and author of *Pen, Ink, & Evidence*. Dr. Nickell and I discussed the text of the book at length and concurred in our concern that the author approached the diary with little skepticism and that too many assumptions were presented as facts without any stated basis. A number of "facts" are incorrect, while several are actually contradicted in other parts of the book. We both believed that simply on the evidence presented in the book, one could only conclude that the diary was a forgery.

An example of a conclusion being reached without any stated basis was the use of the term "one off." The earliest known use of this phrase in America is 1925, and 1934 in England. The editor of the *Oxford English Dictionary* states that he would be "surprised but not dumbfounded if its first use predated 1934 by as much as half a century" (p. 179). An editor of *Webster's* had a similar reaction. Yet after quoting both of these sources by name, the author wrote, "I have also learned of oral uses of the expression in late Victorian times that have not yet found their way into the dictionaries." No sources and no explanation were given for this statement, yet a factor in questioning the authenticity of the text of the diary was summarily dismissed. This was only one of many examples of important statements with no apparent foundation. (It was also quite clear to anyone familiar with Victorian prose that many phrases and uses of words in the diary were not common in the 1880s.)

Some "facts" are contradicted by the book itself. On page 169, the author writes, "Even more striking, the diary also mentions facts of which only the murderer could have been aware. Who else but the Ripper could have known that Catherine Eddowes had an empty tin match box? It is mentioned nowhere prior to the discovery of the diary." But on page 79, Harrison had written that a police list that includes a mention of the tin match box appeared in 1987.

One of the most important pieces of evidence described in the book proved, if one were to accept the "facts" as stated,

202 The "Dear Boss" letter — page one of a genuine letter written to the
Central News Office in London during the Jack the Ripper killings,
above which is shown the Ripper's signature from page two of the letter
(enlarged); it is not known if the letter *is* by Jack the Ripper

that the diary was a hoax. A letter was sent on September 25, 1888, to "The Boss, Central News Office, London" [202]. This letter, genuinely written in 1888 and widely publicized, was signed *Jack the Ripper*, the first use of this name. The letter may or may not have been written by the murderer, but whether it was or not, the diary directly reflected the language found in it. The "Dear Boss" letter was cited on page 87 to prove the diary's authenticity. "The use of language in the letter repeatedly echoes that of the diary. 'Down on whores,' the 'red stuff,' and the 'funny little games' is Maybrick talking. The hollow, sinister, underlined 'ha ha' of the diary and the letter is Maybrick mocking." These and other phrases used in the 1888 letter were also used repeatedly in the diary. Much later in the book (p. 176), Harrison reports that Sue Iremonger, a documents expert consulted by the English publisher in London, "does not link the handwriting of the diary with that of the 'Dear Boss' letter." If Iremonger is correct, there can be only one conclusion: the letter is a forgery. If the letter was in fact written by Jack the Ripper, then the diary, which copies its language but does not match its handwriting, must be forged. If the letter was a hoax of the time, then the diary must still be a forgery since it copies its language.

Having concluded that the text of the book was unreliable and contradictory and that it would be extremely unwise to rely upon any of it as factual, I was especially interested to see the full original reports submitted to the author by the experts hired to prove its authenticity. It is my standard practice always to insist upon seeing the complete files and reports as I may interpret an expert's report differently. This was never more true than in the present case.

Dr. Nicholas Eastaugh had been engaged to do a forensic examination of the ink, and his test was very competently carried out. His finding that there are no elements in the ink that are inconsistent with a date of 1888 is correct, but what was not published was that he stressed, as early as October 1992, that other major tests needed to be done as well. In June 1993, he wrote to the publisher, "I think it would be very dangerous to quote [me] . . . saying I say the ink is Victorian, when I don't — merely that it could be. I also want to underline that I am unwilling to highlight that the ink behaves like the Victorian reference material without the qualifying statement that we cannot actually distinguish it on the basis of solubility from later inks of similar composition, and that the ink of the diary must equally behave like inks applied substantially later than 1889." As recently as August 1993, he was still urging the English publisher to authorize the additional analyses that were necessary. Dr. Eastaugh is also quoted in the book as having "determined that the black dust found in the gutter of the diary was . . . bone black" (p. 174). What he actually reported was, "The black powder is possibly based on bone black." (The significance of bone black was related to the purported author's addiction to arsenic and strychnine.)

Dr. David Forshaw's 59-page report was quoted extensively throughout the book, providing the basis for asserting that from a psychiatric standpoint, this was the diary of a person who shows the personality of a serial killer. (When I inquired about Dr. Forshaw's experience and qualifications as a specialist in serial killers, I was told that his work was confidential and could not be discussed.) The report he submitted to the author/publisher contained two statements that were startling. In the opening of his lengthy report Dr. Forshaw wrote, "Starting from the assumption that the journal is genuine, the aim of this contribution is to come to an understanding of James Maybrick the man, and of the state of mind of Jack the Ripper." Dr. Forshaw clearly did not see his role as authenticating the text as that of a serial killer consistent with the known personality of Jack the Ripper. His role was to explain the text on the basis that it was genuine.

More alarming was the final paragraph of Dr. Forshaw's report. It was crossed out and was not published: "If the journal is genuine then it tells a tragic tale. The account is feasible and indeed makes sense. However, there are other possibilities; it could be a modern or old fake or the product of a deluded mind contemporaneous with the Jack the Ripper murders. In view of the detail of the journal and the insights into the psychopathology of serial killers contained within, it would seem, to me anyway, that the most likely options are that it is either genuine or modern fake. A thorough examination forensic [sic] of the journal itself and of its provence [sic] would be essential components of deciding between the two."

After I read Dr. Forshaw's report, its importance in establishing the diary's likely authenticity was severely diminished. I decided that it would be unnecessary to engage other noted forensic psychiatrists who specialize in serial killers to review the text and report their opinion if this was a text likely written by such a killer, unless further handwriting and forensic examinations showed a likelihood of genuineness.

The historical evidence within the text of a manuscript is always of importance in determining authenticity, and the Harrison book assures the reader that the historical facts within the diary are correct. However, given the inaccuracy of the other chapters in the book, I had no reason to believe that the historical "facts" in the book were any more accurate.

The ideal course would be to have Dr. Nickell, a thorough historical investigator, determine how the text of the diary compared with unpublished and published information about Jack the Ripper as well as information concerning the life of James Maybrick. While Warner Books never hesitated in stating that they would delay publication until all necessary research was done, it appeared that a thorough examination of the handwriting and writing materials would likely be conclusive, and I decided to pursue these examinations first; if they were inconclusive or positive, the accuracy and likelihood of the historical facts in the text could be investigated.

People who have not been involved in major literary forgeries are unaware of the resourcefulness of perpetrators of such hoaxes. In the Ripper case many persons stated that it was too elaborate to be a hoax; they were not aware that virtually everyone said that no one could possibly forge nearly sixty Hitler diaries, nor could anyone create Howard Hughes's autobiography or Benito Mussolini's diaries, nor could a young man in Salt Lake City forge letters and manuscripts whose content would shake the Mormon Church to its foundations. If investigators assume that something is too complex to be a fraud, then they are likely to be deceived. Forgers are not always motivated by money or fame; their goal can be the simple satisfaction of fooling the experts. Knowing the psychology of forgers is almost as important as knowing how to analyze handwriting.

The original diary was brought to Chicago on August 20, 1993, by Robert Smith for the examination of the handwriting, ink, and paper. I met him at the laboratory of Maureen Casey Owens, the former president of the American Society of Questioned Document Examiners, author of numerous papers on forensic handwriting questions, and, for twenty-five years, the Chicago Police Department's expert in document examination. We were joined by Robert L. Kuranz, who has been a research ink chemist for more than thirty years, and Dr. Nickell [203].

My immediate reaction, and, I later learned, that of Mrs. Owens as well as Dr. Nickell, was that the diary was written much more recently than the late 1880s. I was also struck by the uniformity of the writing and ink — highly unusual in a diary — a uniformity that immediately reminded me of my first glimpse of the Hitler diaries.

I was also surprised that the diary was written in a scrapbook, not a normal diary book. Scrapbooks, larger in format and made of very absorbent heavy paper, were used for mounting postcards, photographs, valentines, and other

203 Robert Kuranz, Maureen Owens, Kenneth Rendell and Robert Smith (clockwise from left to right) examining the Jack the Ripper diary

greeting cards, and I had not previously encountered one used as a diary. It was possible but unlikely.

We were all very suspicious of the fact that approximately twenty pages at the beginning of the book had been torn out. There are no logical explanations for the purported author, Maybrick, a man of means, to have torn them out himself. If for some reason he wanted to use a scrapbook for a diary, he would have bought a new one. He would have been unlikely to take one he already had and tear out the contents. It was logical, however, that someone wanting to forge a diary, and not knowing the difference between a scrapbook and diary, would have bought a Victorian scrapbook, torn out the leaves already used, and used those remaining for their fabrication.

In Chicago, the first three forensic tests were undertaken to rule out an unexpected piece of evidence (such as the wrong fluorescent color in the Mormon case): ultraviolet and infra-red examinations and a test for the slightest impressions in the paper (electronic static detection analysis). The ultraviolet examination showed that rectangular pieces, probably post-cards, were mounted on the first, now missing page (an outline of their images appear on the first existing page). It also showed no age offset of the ink in the diary. In many instances, ink on one page will create an impression on the facing page it is in contact with, especially if they have been in contact for over one hundred years. This age effect of the ink is rarely visible without the aid of ultraviolet light.

The diary was then photographed using a large camera so that very accurate photographs could be studied after the diary was taken back to London. Afterwards, everyone examined the diary, studying it through a stereo microscope, observing ink and pen strokes. A number of ink core samples were taken by Robert Kuranz using an instrument similar to a hypodermic needle. Tiny samples of the ink and underlying paper were then put into capsules for detailed scientific analysis the following week.

While the ink and paper samplings were taking place, Maureen Owens, Dr. Nickell, and I met outside the labora-tory. All of us agreed that there was no evidence, at that point, to indicate this was a genuine Victorian diary of anyone. There were the serious questions of the scrapbook itself, the uniformity of the entries supposedly written over a period of more than a year, and a style of writing not used in Victorian England.

We had also been studying a full-size color photograph of the "Dear Boss" letter (mentioned earlier), and none of us could see any relationship to the handwriting in the diary.

We agreed that a very detailed analysis and comparison of the diary and letter should be undertaken, as well as a study of the possibility of someone disguising his handwriting in the "Dear Boss" letter. We would also study the uniformity of the writing, a circumstance that was inconsistent with a diary. Different entries should be written with different starts of the writing; a diary would always be placed at a slightly different angle relative to the writer each time a new entry was made. Also, each new entry should begin with a new supply of ink on the steel-nibbed pen. With this type of writing instrument, it is impossible to have the same quantity of ink distributed onto the paper if there has been an interruption between entries. If the amount of ink on the pen at the end of one day's entry is the same as that at the beginning of the next day's entry, then they were written at the same time.

Smith had also brought with him photocopies of Maybrick's marriage certificate bearing an unquestioned genuine signature, as well as photocopies of his will, which he indicated was considered to be a forgery, probably by Maybrick's brother, Michael. (The Harrison book indicates both that it is genuine [p. 126] and "possibly" genuine [p. 176].)

During the following week, Robert Kuranz used thin-layer chromatographic techniques to analyze the ink for any elements that would be inconsistent with the date and found none (in this, he basically duplicated the work of Dr. Eastaugh). We had not expected to find any elements that would date the ink as recent but could not rule out the possibility. (It is relatively easy today to make ink with the elements that were used in Victorian England.)

Five of the ink/paper samples extracted by Robert Kuranz had meanwhile been sent to Rod McNeil, a forensic scientist who had developed the ion migration test, to determine how long the ink had been on the paper. We had some concern that the nature of the book, a scrapbook with relatively more absorbent paper, might make this analysis more difficult.

Both Maureen Owens and I continued to work on the handwriting, and it became increasingly evident that the examination of the handwriting would be conclusive in itself. We had determined that the "Dear Boss" letter was definitely not written by the same person who wrote the diary (the same conclusion the English publisher's handwriting expert, Sue Iremonger, had arrived at). The only question concerning the "Dear Boss" letter was whether it was possible for the diary's author to have disguised his or her own writing by adopting a different style. Mrs. Owens has two and a half decades of experience in detecting situations in which a person is attempting to write in a manner to cover up his own handwriting. She was definite in her opinion that this was not the case with the "Dear Boss" letter. This analysis alone was sufficient to prove the diary a forgery.

Our further examination of the writing in the diary confirmed what Mrs. Owens and I suspected the first time we saw the diary: the writing was not consistent with letter formations of the late 1880s; there was a uniformity of ink and slant of writing in going from one entry to the next (supposedly written at different times) that was unnatural and very indicative of a forger writing multiple entries at one time. A lack of variation in layout also led to the same conclusion.

Most important of all, a careful examination of Maybrick's will conclusively showed that the signature on the will was signed by the same person who signed the marriage certificate — James Maybrick — and that the text of the will was also written by Maybrick. This was an unexpected development, as Robert Smith had stated that there was very strong evidence it was written by Maybrick's brother, Michael. (Smith and I never produced this evidence; in fact, Charles Hamilton had, in his own collection, a three-page letter of Michael Maybrick which conclusively proved he did not write his brother's will.)

An analysis and comparison of the Maybrick will with the Jack the Ripper diary conclusively showed that they were written by two different persons. Both examples were supposedly written at the same time. There was sufficient evidence to reach a definitive conclusion. The historical facts in the diary so clearly identify the author as James Maybrick that proof that he did not write the diary left only the conclusion that it was a hoax.

Every area of examination indicated or proved the diary was a hoax. There was no reason to believe it was genuine; nothing was indicative of a genuine Victorian diary, and two critical handwriting comparisons showed it to be a forgery.

A meeting was immediately held at the office of Warner Books in New York City, and they issued a press statement announcing they would cancel publication. The possibility of Warner publishing the book as fiction was not considered, but those present believed that Smith, with enormous financial gain at stake, would refuse to believe my report just as he had ignored the statements of his own experts. Several days later Rob McNeil's test of the ion migration of the ink, used by the FBI and Secret Service, showed the diary to have been written in the twentieth century.

Robert Smith's reaction was predictable. He had not listened to his own experts, and there was no reason to believe he would listen to us. He responded with a series of contradictory and confusing statements, not answering the points in our report but presenting "new evidence," most remarkably, a watch that he said would now "prove" the diary to have been written by Jack the Ripper.

Smith also claimed that his experts supported the diary's authenticity, but a week later a London court voided the secrecy agreements they had signed with him. Smith's experts contradicted his statements, either declaring the diary was a hoax, or that their work was incomplete and inconclusive. The lawsuit that prompted the court order had been brought by the *Sunday Times* of London, which had purchased serialization rights from Smith.

Two weeks after the release of our report for Time-Warner, the *Sunday Times* of London published its own report, confirming all of our findings and opinions as well as discussing in detail the historical accuracy of the facts in the diary. They concluded, "there are serious discrepancies between the diary and the known facts about both James Maybrick and Jack the Ripper." A number of authors of books on Jack the Ripper were quoted in the newspaper's report, and contrary to what Smith had been claiming, they all stated that it was their opinion that the diary was a hoax.

Not unexpectedly, Smith went ahead with publication in England, changing the dust jacket to indicate that the authenticity was controversial and that the readers could decide for themselves. Quite unexpectedly, the Walt Disney publishing subsidiary, Hyperion, decided to publish the book in the United States. They did this with full knowledge of our report for Time-Warner, which they published in the back of the book, and of the *Sunday Times* of London's report, which they claimed they did not have time to include. They were also aware of the statements by Smith's experts but claimed not to have time to include these either. They did, however, have the time and space for Smith to write a rebuttal to my report. Although Hyperion represented the authenticity of the Jack the Ripper diary as a subject of debate, it was a debate with all of the experts on one side and merely the English publisher and the author on the other.

As of this writing, the question still remains as to who actually wrote this diary. Most believe it was written very recently, probably within the year before its announced "discovery."

10
Equipment Used in Questioned Document Examinations

A person experienced in examining historical letters and documents, with a good knowledge of forgery detection techniques, will develop a trained eye that will identify the overwhelming majority of forgeries with no more than a ten power magnifying glass. The equipment described here is necessary, in varying degrees, in dealing with only a small percentage of forgeries, but these are the more sophisticated and difficult to detect.

THE MICROSCOPE

The microscope is the most fundamental and useful piece of equipment used in document examination. While many of the determinations necessary in examining documents can be accomplished with a ten power magnifying glass, a stereoptic variable power microscope is much more convenient and has available much higher magnifications for situations in which they are required [204]. It is important to have a wide range of powers available; lower magnifications, showing a much larger section of writing, are important in observing overall letter writing patterns and most particularly in examining an entire letter to determine if there are any indications of forgery. The very narrow field of view through a magnifying glass makes this more difficult.

Variable power, increased or decreased by turning a dial, makes it possible to focus in on one section of writing without losing perspective on how the section was written. At higher magnifications it is easy to become "lost" while viewing a tiny section of writing, and it is a great aid to be able to lower the magnification, see the overall word or letter, and then return to the higher magnification.

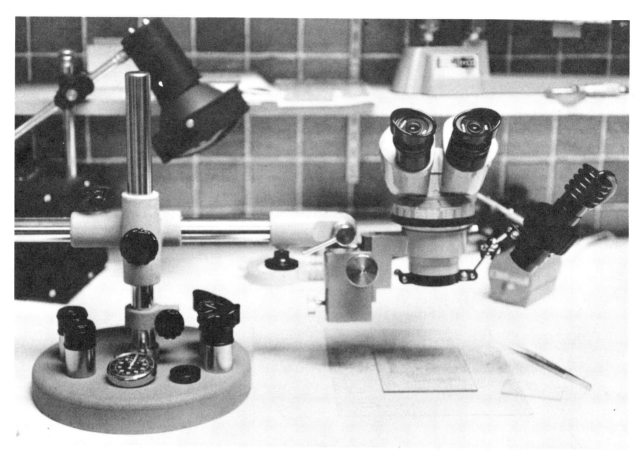

204 A stereoptic variable power microscope capable of enlargements from eight to one hundred times

Higher magnifications are unnecessary in examining very good facsimiles and also in determining such factors as how a pen was held while writing and if the position of the writer changed, the direction of writing, and type of writing instrument.

The microscope that I use can be varied from 8 times to 100 times, and I have found this range to be more than adequate. The body is on a long arm so that it can be extended over a document and it is fitted with a high-intensity spotlight that is used to illuminate the area being viewed and also has the capability of being used at varying angles to the paper to create different viewing effects. (I have found circular lamps mounted on the base of the microscope to be less satisfactory.) One of the main uses of a spotlight held at a low angle to the paper is the detection of erasures; by illuminating the side of the paper fiber, areas of abrasion become quite apparent. Faint pencil writing can also be more visible when illuminated in this way.

205 A high-pressure mercury arc lamp

TRANSMITTED LIGHT

Transmitted light, that is, light coming through the paper from the verso, will also show areas where the paper has been thinned by erasures as well as make the observation of watermarks quite convenient. Differences in the thickness of the ink (where one line crosses over another), or a character that has been retouched or rewritten over, are more readily and clearly seen in some cases with transmitted light.

ULTRAVIOLET LIGHT

Ultraviolet light is less frequently used but can show very useful results in some situations. My own experience is that a high-pressure mercury arc lamp is necessary for worthwhile results and that the lamps of lesser intensity, although more easily available, are relatively ineffective in examining documents [205]. Examination with ultraviolet light will cause many papers and inks to fluoresce, and it therefore has the added use of making faded writing appear much stronger, a very helpful tool when cataloging faded and difficult to read material. Like the other light sources, ultraviolet light will cause different sections of paper to fluoresce differently if a section has been erased. When it is suspected that a forged section may have been added to a genuine document, a fairly common technique, the ultraviolet light will usually distinguish between similar-appearing inks; apparently identical pieces of paper may also be distinguished. Adhesives also fluoresce in most cases, and a postage stamp applied to a forgery to create an appearance of authenticity will usually fluoresce two different colors because of the two different adhesives used. Ultraviolet examination frequently confirms that all of the material components are identical, and this in itself is important information if a forgery is suspected.

INFRARED RADIATION

Infrared radiation equipment is more complex, and its application to forgery detection is not as great as the ultraviolet light. Its use is mainly in making visible faded or mostly erased pencil writing and certain types of inks.

TEST PLATES

Test plates made of glass with etched lines are very useful in making comparisons of handwriting and are necessary in examining typewriting [206-208]. These plates can be placed over the writing being examined and the quality of the etched lines is such that they can be used in conjunction with the microscope. The plates used in comparing handwritings very quickly aid the examiner in noticing habits of writing. By placing a plate with lines of varying degrees of slant over writing, consistent patterns of slanting become apparent, as do exceptions to the standard degree of slanting. (It can also be determined if a writer was consistently in the same position relative to the paper when writing; this would be of significance in examining a questioned diary, where entries would have been written on different days and different locations; consistent slanting in such a diary would be highly unusual.)

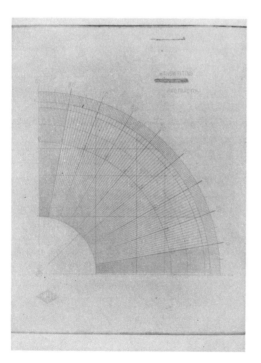

206 A protractor used for handwriting comparisons

Letters or combinations of letters that are written above or below an imaginary baseline are quickly observed. Measuring plates finely etched with divisions from 1/10 to 1/1000 of an inch make it possible to determine the width of pen nibs, or to precisely compare two supposedly identical postal markings by exactly determining the width and size of each component.

Comparisons of typewriting examples are facilitated with typewriting test plates. Examining all of the characters using a grid pattern plate will quickly determine characters out of alignment with each other, the baseline, or slant. For extensive work with typewriting it is necessary to have test plates for each of the American and European typefaces and sizes.

207
A protractor used for comparisons
in typewriting (left)

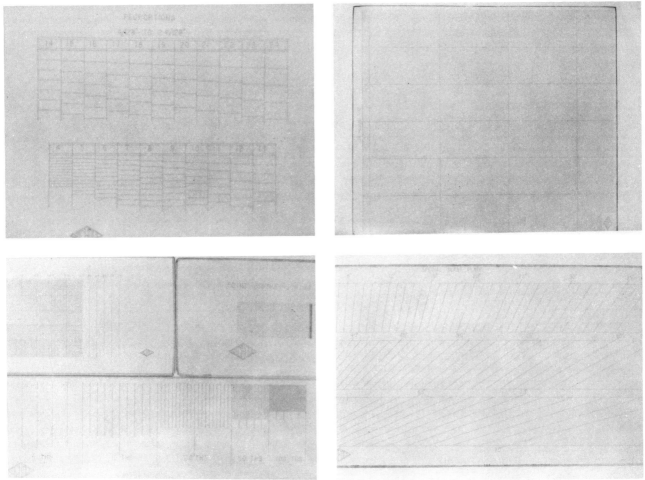

208a-d Various handwriting test plates

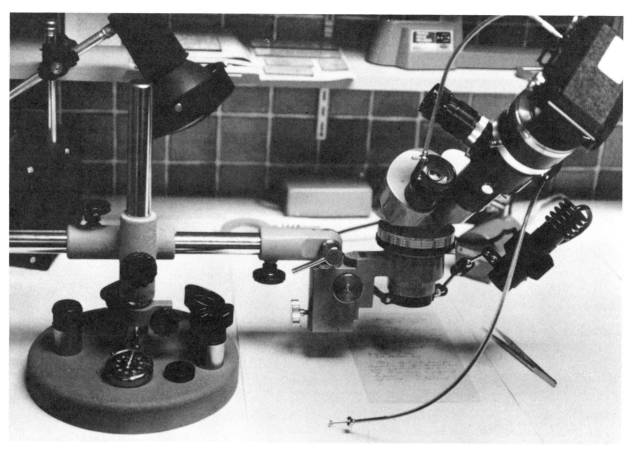

209 A Nikon microscope camera
attached to a microscope

THE MICRONOMETER

The thickness of paper can be determined with a
micronometer, but its applications are very limited. Older
paper naturally varies in thickness, and it therefore only has
an application in comparing paper of recent origin.

PHOTOGRAPHY

Photography through a microscope is accomplished with a
microscope camera [209]. All of the illustrations in this book
were made with a Nikon microscope camera attached to the
microscope.

A Selected Bibliography

FACSIMILES

Albrecht, Otto Edwin, Herbert Cahoon, and Douglas C. Ewing. *The Mary Flagler Cary Music Collection: Printed Books and Music, Manuscripts, Autograph Letters, Documents, Portraits.* New York: Pierpont Morgan Library, 1970.

_____. "Musical Treasures in the Morgan Library." *Notes* 18 (June 1972): 643-651.

Anmann, R. *Die Handschrift de Kunstler.* Bern: H. Huben, [1953].

Autograph Letters & Manuscripts: Major Acquisitions of the Pierpont Morgan Library, 1924-1974. New York: Pierpont Morgan Library, 1974.

Berard, Auguste Simon Louis, et al. *Isographie des hommes célèbres, ou collection de facsimile de lettres autographes et de signatures.* 4 volumes. Paris: 1828-1843; *Supplement* by Etienne Charavay, 1880.

British Autography. A Collection of Facsimilies of the Hand Writing of Royal and Illustrious Personages, with their Authentic Portraits. 3 volumes. London: J. Thane.

Brotherhead, William, ed. *The Book of the Signers: Containing Facsimile Letters of the Signers of the Declaration of Independence.* Philadelphia: W. Brotherhead, 1861.

Cahoon, Herbert, Thomas V. Lange, and Charles A. Ryskamp. *American Literary Autographs from Washington Irving to Henry James.* New York: Dover Publications, in association with the Pierpont Morgan Library, 1977.

Camner, James, and Neale Lanigan, Jr. *Film Autographs 1894-1941.* James Camner, 1978.

Carr, Paul K. *The Autographs of President Gerald R. Ford.* New York: Universal Autograph Collectors Club, 1974.

Casoni, Frederick. *The Handwriting of Richard M. Nixon.* Rockville Centre: Universal Autograph Collectors Club, 1982.

Charavay, Etienne. *Catalogue de la précieuse collection d'autographes composant le cabinet de M. Alfred Bovet* . 3 volumes. Paris: E. Charavay, 1884-1885. One of the most important facsimile works for European material.

_____. *Inventaire des Autographes et des Documents Historiques Composant la Collection M. Benjamin Fillon.* Paris: Etienne Charavay and Frederic Naylor, 1877.

Croft, Peter J. *Autograph Poetry in the English Language.* 2 volumes. New York: McGraw-Hill, 1973.

Czwiklitzer, Christophe. *Lettres Autographes de Peintres et Sculpteurs du XVe Siècle à Nos Jours*. Basel: Editions Art-C.C., 1976.

Dawson, Giles Edwin, and Laetitia Kennedy-Skipton. *Elizabethan Handwriting*. New York: Norton, [1966].

Fairbank, Alfred John, and Berthold Wolpe. *Renaissance Handwriting*. London: Faber and Faber, [1960].

Friendenthall, Richard. *Letters of Great Artists from Ghiberti to Gainsborough and Letters of the Great Artists from Blake to Pollock*. London: Thames and Hudson, 1963.

Geigy-Hagenback, Karl. *Album von Handschriften Berühmter Personlichkeiten vom Mittelater bis zur Neuzeit*. 1925. A very comprehensive reference work of facsimiles of European signatures.

Gerstenberg, Walter, and Martin Hürlimann, eds. *Musiker Handschriften. 2* volumes. Zurich: Atlantis Verlag, 1960-1961. English edition translated by Ernst Roth.

_____. *Composers' Autographs. 2* volumes. Teaneck, N.J.: Fairleigh Dickinson University Press, 1968.

Grasbergerger, Franz. *Die Handschriften der Meister: Berühmte Werke der Tonkunst im Autograph*. Vienna: Gesellschaft der Musikfreunde, 1966.

_____. *Kostbarkeiten der Musik. I: Das Lied*. Tutzing, Germany: Hans Schneider, 1968.

Grebanier, Bernard D. N. *The Great Shakespeare Forgery*. New York: Norton, 1965.

Greg, Walter Wilson. *English Literary Autographs, 1550-1650*. 3 volumes. Oxford: Oxford University Press, 1925-1932. Reprint. Nendeln, Liechtenstein: Kraus Reprint, 1968.

Grieve, Hilda Elizabeth Poole. *Examples of English Handwriting, 1150-1750*. [Essex, England]: Essex Education Committee, 1974.

Hamilton, Charles. *American Autographs*. 2 volumes. Norman: University of Oklahoma Press, 1983. The definitive selection of facsimile examples of American presidents and a wide-ranging selection of facsimiles of participants in the American Revolution, as well as illustrations of secretarial and forged signatures.

_____. *The Book of Autographs*. New York: Simon & Schuster, 1978.

_____. *Leaders and Personalities of the Third Reich: Their Biographies, Portraits, and Autographs*. San Jose, Calif.: R. James Bender Publishing, 1984. A comprehensive collection of facsimiles of Third Reich personalities.

_____. *The Signature of America*. New York: Harper & Row, 1979. One of the most comprehensive books of facsimiles of signatures.

Hardy, William John. *The Handwriting of the Kings and Queens of England*. [London]: Religious Tract Society, 1893.

Hector, Leonard Charles. *The Handwriting of English Documents*. 2d ed. London: E. Arnold, 1966.

Hurlimann, Martin. *Musiker-Handschriften: Zeugins des Zurcher Musiklebens*. Zurich: Atlantis Verlag, 1969.

Jans, Hans Jorg, ed. *Musiker-Handschriften: Original Partituren aus der Sammlung Dr. Paul Sacher*. Lucerne: Bartschi & Hasler, 1973.

Jenkinson, Hilary. *Paleography and the Practical Study of the Court Hand*. Cambridge: Cambridge University Press, 1915.

Johnson, Charles. *English Court Hand, A.D. 1066 to 1500*. Oxford: Clarendon Press, 1915.

Klinkenborg, Verlyn, Herbert Cahoon, and Charles Ryskamp. *British Literary Manuscripts, Series I from 800 to 1800*. New York: Dover Publications, 1981.

Leigh, Owen H., ed. *Universal Classic Manuscripts*. 2 volumes.

Lescure, M. de. *Les autographes et le gout des autographes en France et à l'étranger*. Paris: V. Gay, 1865.

Lesure, François, and Nanie Bridgman. *Collection musicale Andre Meyer: Manuscrits, autographes, musique imprimée et manuscrit*. Abbeville: F. Paillart, [1960].

Marans, M. Wesley. *Sincerely Yours*. Boston: Little, Brown and Company, 1983.

Mare, A. C. de la. *The Handwriting of Italian Humanists*. Oxford: Oxford University Press, 1973.

Morrison, Alfred. *Catalogue of the Collection of Autograph Letters and Historical Documents formed between 1865 and 1882*. 6 volumes. London: Strangeways & Sons, 1883. One of the most important facsimile reference works.

Nash, Ray. *American Penmanship 1800-1850: A History of Writing and Bibliography of Copybooks from Jenkins to Spencer*. Worcester, Mass.: American Antiquarian Society, 1969.

Netherclift, Joseph. *Autograph Letters, Characteristic Extracts, and Signatures, from the Correspondence of Illustrious and Distinguished Women of Great Britain, from the XIVth to the XIXth Century*. [London: J. Netherclift], 1838.

[Nicolas, Alain]. *Souverains et Chefs d'Etat Français*. Paris: Les Neuf Muses.

Nichols, John G. *Autographs of Royal, Noble, Learned, and Remarkable Personages Conspicuous in English History*. London: J. B. Nichols and Son, 1829.

Osley, A. S. *Scribes and Sources*. Boston: David R. Godine, 1980.

Petti, Anthony G. *English Literary Hands from Chaucer to Dryden*. London: Edward Arnold, 1977.

Poetry, Famous Verse Manuscripts: Facsimiles of Original Manuscripts as Submitted to Poetry. [Chicago]: Poetry, 1954.

Rawlins, Ray. *Four Hundred Years of British Autographs*. London: J. M. Dent, 1970.

_____. *The Guinness Book of World Autographs*. Enfield, Middlesex, England: Guinness Superlatives, Ltd., 1977.

Reese II, Michael. *Autographs of the Confederacy*. New York: Cohasco, 1981.

Rendell, Kenneth W. *The American Frontier, from the Atlantic to the Pacific*. 3 volumes. 1,000 letters, documents, printed books, broadsides, pamphlets, maps, and other items representing virtually all major figures concerned with the exploration and crossing of the Rocky Mountains, the settlement and annexation of Texas, the California Gold Rush, cowboys and Indians, and the settlement of the west. Kenneth W. Rendell, 1980.

_____. *The Medieval World, 800-1450.* A comprehensive catalog of letters, documents, illuminated leaves, and manuscripts, both secular and religious, representing various aspects of life and society during the Middle Ages. Kenneth W. Rendell, 1979.

_____. *Renaissance Europe, 1450-1600.* 270 letters, manuscripts, documents, printed books, bindings, maps, and woodcuts documenting life in Renaissance Europe and representing most of the major political and religious figures of the period. Kenneth W. Rendell, 1979.

_____. *Autograph Letters, Manuscripts, Drawings—French Artists & Authors.* Kenneth W. Rendell, 1977.

Stevens, Benjamin Franklin. *Facsimiles of Manuscripts in European Archives Relating to America, 1773-1783.* 24 volumes. London: Malby & Sons, 1889-1895. Reprint (25 volumes). Washington, Del.: Mellifont Press, 1970.

Tannenbaum, Samuel A. *The Handwriting of the Renaissance.* New York: Columbia University Press, 1930. Reprint. New York: Frederick Ungar Publishing Co., 1967.

Taylor, John M. *From the White House Inkwell: American Presidential Autographs.* Rutland, Vt: Charles E. Tuttle Co., 1968.

Thomas, George C. *Autograph Letters and Autographs of the Signers of the Declaration of Independence.* Philadelphia: Privately printed, 1908.

Thompson, H. Keith, and Henry Strutz. *Doenitz at Nuremberg: A Re-appraisal.* New York: Ambler, 1977.

Warner, Sir George Frederick, ed. *Facsimiles of Royal, Historical, Literary and Other Autographs in the Department of Manuscripts, British Museum.* London: British Museum, 1809.

_____. *Universal Classic Manuscripts.* London/Washington, D.C.: M. W. Dunne, 1901.

William, Henry Smith. *The History of the Art of Writing.* London: Hooper & Jackson, [1902].

Winkler, E. W. *Manuscript Letters and Documents of Early Texians 1821-1845.* Austin: Steck Company, 1937.

Winsor, Justin. *Narrative and Critical History of America.* 8 volumes. Boston: Houghton Mifflin, 1884-1889.

Winternitz, Emanuel. *Musical Autographs from Monteverdi to Hindemith.* 2 volumes. Princeton: Princeton University Press, 1955.

Wright, C. E. *English Vernacular Hands from the Twelfth to the Fifteenth Centuries.* Oxford: Clarendon Press, 1960.

FORGERIES

Charavay, Etienne. *Faux autographes: Affaire Vrain-Lucas; étude critique sur la collection vendue à M. Chel Chasles et observations sur les moyens de reconnaître les faux autographes.* Paris: J. Charavay, 1870.

Clements, William L. Library. *Facsimiles & Forgeries: A Guide to a Timely Exhibition*. Ann Arbor, Mich.: Clements Library, 1950.

Conway, James V. P. *Evidential Documents*. Springfield, Ill.: Charles Thomas, 1959.

Farrer, James A. *Literary Forgeries*. London: Longmans, Green and Co., 1907.

Grant, J. *Books and Documents*. New York: Chemical Publishing Company of New York, 1937.

Hamilton, Charles. *Great Forgers and Famous Fakes*. New York: Crown Publishers, 1980. While this work does not deal with the detection of forgeries, its numerous illustrations make it an important work in the field.

_____. *The Robot that Helped to Make a President*. New York, 1965. The first book on autopen signatures; a classic.

Harris, Robert. *Selling Hitler*. London: Faber and Faber, 1986. A detailed history of the Hitler diaries fraud inside *Stern* magazine and also at the *Sunday Times* of London.

Harrison, Wilson R. *Suspect Documents: Their Scientific Examination*. London: Sweet and Maxwell, 1958. A standard reference work.

_____. *Forgery Detection: A Practical Guide*. New York: Praeger, 1963. A standard reference work.

Haselden, Reginald Betti. *Scientific Aids for the Study of Manuscripts*. Oxford: Oxford University Press for the Bibliographical Society, 1935.

Hector, Leonard Charles. *Paleography and Forgery*. York, England: St. Anthony's Press, 1959.

Hilton, Ordway. *Scientific Examination of Questioned Documents*. Chicago: Callaghan & Company, 1956.

Lindsey, Robert. *A Gathering of Saints*. New York, 1988. The best and most comprehensive account of the Mormon murders and fraud written by the *New York Times* correspondent, generally considered to represent the Mormon Church in the fairest light.

Myers, Robin, and Michael Harris, eds. *Fakes and Frauds: Varieties of Deception in Print and Manuscript*. Detroit: Omnigraphics, 1989. A small but excellent general work with an important chapter by Nicholas Barker on the forgery of the "Oath of a Freeman."

Naifeh, Steven, and Gregory White-Smith. *The Mormon Murders*. New York, 1988. Reviews of this book have heavily criticized it for being factually wrong in literally hundreds of cases. While *Salamander* (Sillitoe) staunchly defends the Mormon Church and its members and attacks everyone else, this work simply attacks everyone involved.

Rapport, Leonard. "Fakes and Facsimiles: Problems of Identification." *The American Archivist* 42, no. 1 (January 1979): 13-58.

Sillitoe, Linda, and Alan Roberts. *Salamander*. Salt Lake City: Signature Books, 1988. A lengthy account of the Mormon murders and fraud written by the reporters for the Mormon Church's newspaper and two others connected with the Mormon Church. While well researched in some ways, this book has been heavily criticized as having been commissioned by the church to defend its role in the case.

Tanner, Jerald. *Tracking the White Salamander*. Salt Lake City: Utah Lighthouse Ministry, [1986].

GENERAL

Benjamin, Mary A. *Autographs: A Key to Collecting*. New York: R. R. Bowker, 1946; rev. ed., 1963. A standard reference work.

Berkeley, Edmund, Jr., Herbert E. Klingelhofer, and Kenneth W. Rendell. *Autographs and Manuscripts: A Collector's Manual*. New York: Charles Scribner's Sons, 1978. The standard and most comprehensive reference work in the field.

Gaur, Albertine. *A History of Writing*. London: The British Library, 1984.

Hamilton, Charles. *Collecting Autographs and Manuscripts*. Norman: University of Oklahoma Press, 1961.

WRITING MATERIALS

Briquet, Charles Moise. *Les Filigranes*. Amsterdam: Paper Publications Society, 1968. The standard reference work on watermarks.

Carvalho, David N. *Forty Centuries of Ink, or a Chronological Narrative Concerning Ink and Its Background*. New York: Banks Law Publishing Co., 1904.

Heawood, Edward. *Watermarks, Mainly of the 17th and 18th Centuries*. Hilversum, Netherlands: Paper Publications Society, 1950.

Hunter, Dard. *Old Papermaking*. [Chillicothe, Ohio: The Author], 1923.

_____. *Papermaking: The History and Technique of an Ancient Craft*. New York: Knopf, 1943.

_____. *Papermaking by Hand in America*. Chillicothe, Ohio: Mountain House Press, 1950.

Mitchell, Charles Ainsworth. *Inks, Their Composition and Manufacture*. 4th ed., rev. London: C. Griffin, [1937].

Nickell, Joe. *Pen, Ink, & Evidence*. Lexington: University Press of Kentucky, 1990.

Reed, Ronald. *The Nature and Making of Parchment*. Leeds, England: Elmete Press, 1976.

Shorter, Alfred H. *Paper Mills and Paper Makers in England, 1495-1800*. Hilversum, Holland: Paper Publications Society, 1957.

Stevenson, Allan Henry. *Paper as Bibliographical Evidence*. London: Bibliographical Society, 1962.

Waters, C. E. *Inks*. Circular C426 of the National Bureau of Standards, U.S. Department of Commerce. Washington, D.C.: Government Printing Office, 1940.

Weeks, Lynan Horace. *A History of Paper-Manufacturing in the United States, 1960-1916*. New York: Lockwood Trade Journal Company, 1916.

Index

letter written and signed by his mother, **178**

secretarial signatures of, 102

Remington, Frederic
  forgeries by Field II of, **24-25,** 62
  forgeries of, 16

Rendell, Kenneth W.
  examines Hitler diaries, reveals hoax, 107, 119-123
  examines Hofmann forgeries, 137-138
  examines Jack the Ripper diary, reveals hoax, 143, 150-154, **203**
  featured in *Stern* article, **184**

Revere, Paul, forgery by Hofmann of, 140, **198**

Rittenhouse, David
  autograph of, **105**
  forgery by Cosey of, 69, **100, 106**

Roosevelt, Franklin D.
  autographs of, **170**
  facsimiles of, **75d**
  secretarial signatures of, 98, **169**

Roosevelt, Theodore
  autograph of, **155**
  secretarial signatures of, 96, **157**
  stamped signatures of, 96, **156**

Rosenthal, Albi, 64

Rubinstein, Anton, feathering of ink in forgery of, 28, **44-45**

Schulte-Hillen, Gerd
  decides to authenticate, publish diaries, 112
  does not question authenticity of Hitlers diaries when he succeeded Fischer, 112

Scott, Sir Walter, forgeries by Antique Smith of, 55-56, **56, 87**

Secrétaires de main, 90, **144**

Secretarial signatures, 90-104

Shakespeare, William, forgeries by Ireland of, 53, **84**

Shankey, A.G., signs for Herbert Hoover, 97, **167-168**

Shaw, George Bernard, forgery of, 8, **8**

Sheets, Gary, murder of his wife, 136

Shelley, Percy Bysshe, forgeries by Major Byron of, 53, 55

Sheridan, Richard Brinsley, 53

Smith, "Antique"
  forgeries by, 55-56, **56, 86-87**
  forgeries of Burns by, 83, **132, 133b-143b**

Smith Gryphon Publishers. *See* Jack the Ripper diary; Smith, Robert

Smith, Joseph, 125-129, 133
  forgery by Hofmann of, 126-127

Smith, Robert
  English publisher of Jack the Ripper diary, 142, 150, **203**
  questions authenticity of Maybrick will, 152-153
  reaction to hoax, 154

Socrates, forgery of Letters of, i

Spring, Robert
  forgeries by, 58
  forgeries of Washington by, 58, 79, **88, 119-120, 121b-130b**

Steel pens, 32, **49-50**

Steifel, Fritz
  acquired Nazi forgeries from Kujau, 109
  owner of Hitler diaries, 108

"Stern/Heidemann dossier," 113, 115

Stern magazine. *See* Hitler diaries

Stevenson, Robert Louis, facsimiles of, **76g**

Taft, William Howard
  autograph of, **158**
  secretarial signature of, 96, **159**

Tennyson, Lord Alfred
  forgeries of, **29d-e**
  involved in exposure of Major Byron as forger, 55

Thackeray, William Makepeace
  "blotter effect" in forgery of, 28, **41**
  interchangeable hands of, 44, **76**

Themistocles, forgery of Letters of, i

Throckmorton, George, 128, 140

Time. See Hitler diaries

Time-Warner. *See* Warner Books

Transmitted light, 157

Trevor-Roper, Hugh
  makes statement on Hitler diaries, 114-115
  praises diaries' importance, retracts statement, 121

Truman, Harry S.
  autographs of, 99, **171**
  facsimiles of, **75e**
  secretarial signatures of, 99, **172**

Twain, Mark. *See* Clemens, Samuel L.

Typewriting
  development and methods used in dating of, 48-50
  idiosyncracies of mechanical typewriters, **79-83a-f**
  test plates for, 158-159, **207**

Ultraviolet light, 157, **205**

Vellum. *See* Paper

Victoria I, facsimiles of, **75b**

Volkischer Beobachter, 21
  used as source of information for Hitler diaries, 115

Vortigern and Rowena, ii, 53

Vrain-Lucas, Denis, forgeries by, 57

Wagner, Richard
  autographs of, **6, 9a**
  forgeries of, 1, **7, 9b**

Walde, Thomas, gives Heidemann approval to pursue Hitler diaries, 109

Warner Books
  asks Kenneth Rendell to authenticate Jack the Ripper diary, 142
  cancels publication, 153
  plans publication of Jack the Ripper diary, 142

Washington, George
  autographs of, **3, 9a,** 77, **117-118, 121a-130a**
  forgeries of, 1, **2, 9b, 29a-b**
  forgeries by Spring of, 58, 79, **88, 119-120, 121b-130b**
  forgery written with a steel pen, 32, **33, 50**
  inappropriate use of vellum in forgery of, 24, **33**

Watermarks in Paper in Holland, England, France (Churchill), 23

Watermarks. *See* Paper

Weinberg, Gerhard, authenticates Hitler diaries for *Newsweek,* 118-119

Weisberg, Charles, forgeries by, 61, **91**

White Salamander letter
  creation by Hofmann of, 126, 128
  importance of, 129
  purchase by Christensen, 134
  purported provenance and examination of, 129
  shown as evidence at Hofmann trail, **189**

Whitman, Walt, forgeries by Weisberg of, 61

Williams, William Carlos, forgeries by McNamara of, 65, **97**

Wilson, Woodrow
  autograph of, **160**
  stamped signature of, 96, **161**

Wood pulp paper, 22

Wordsworth, Mary, signs for her husband William Wordsworth, 95, **151**

Wordsworth, William
  autograph of, **152**
  secretarial signatures by his wife, Mary Wordsworth, 95, **151**

Wove paper, 22, **31**

Writing Instruments, 32-33. *See also* Ballpoint pens; Defective pens; Felt tip pens; Mechanical pencils; Pencils; Quill pens; Steel pens

ABOUT THE AUTHOR

Kenneth Rendell began collecting historical letters and documents in the mid-1950s. In 1959, he became a dealer, which enabled him to examine and handle many pieces outside his own collecting areas.

Rendell has been a consultant in authenticity and fair market value to the Library of Congress, the National Archives, and virtually every major library and museum in the United States and Canada. He has testified in court as an expert witness for both the FBI and the IRS and has the distinction of winning the only two U.S. Tax Court cases that were decided without compromise (one on behalf of the taxpayer, the other for the IRS). He has also regularly presented papers and lectures on authenticity and establishment of fair market value at the annual meetings of the Society of American Archivists, the American Library Association, the Association of College and Research Libraries, the Manuscript Society, the Antiquarian Booksellers Association, and the International League of Autograph and Manuscript Dealers.

He has written numerous articles for trade magazines and scholarly journals and dozens of works on collecting in specialized areas. He is co-editor of two books sponsored by the Manuscript Society, one of which was honored by the American Library Association as an outstanding reference work. In addition, he is the author of *A Guide to Collecting Historical Letters and Documents* (Norman: University Oklahoma Press, 1994), the standard reference work in the field.

Forgery detection is the most fundamental part of dealing in historical letters and documents. In addition to authenticating the material he offers for sale, Rendell has worked as a consultant to *Newsweek*, Time-Warner, and CBS News in major forgery cases. His role in exposing the Mussolini diaries, the Hitler diaries, the Mormon forgeries, and the Jack the Ripper diary is chronicled in the present work.

Rendell's research and administrative offices are in Boston (P.O. Box 9001, Wellesley, MA 02181). His two galleries (989 Madison Ave., New York, NY 10021, and 309 N. Beverly Dr., Beverly Hills, CA 90210) offer the world's most diverse selection of historical letters and documents framed with portraits. Monthly catalogs of both framed and unframed pieces are available.